CW00739989

HOW TO BECOME A MILLIONAIRE ENTREPRENEUR STARTING FROM SCRATCH

Dario Abate

HOW2
EDIZIONI

SUMMARY

PREFACE: THE NEW PRINCE or "There's an endless potential out there..."

Behind false moralisms, Dario Abate takes craftily control of the situation, saying **what and what not to do to become rich.** In other words, as Niccolò Machiavelli did with his *Prince*, the author suggests the entrepreneur to leave scruples to someone else. Abate does that using so direct tones that, sometimes, they can be cruel, but it's the cruelty necessary to whom that want to take the bull by the horns.

Learn how to:

- realize your dreams economically
- achieve the indispensable qualities for the perfect entrepreneur
- become a wishful thinker entrepreneur
- do not let others limit you
- define your entrepreneurial project
- get your startup off the ground
- exploit marketing resources
- find funds for starting your business
- interpret people needs
- know the new big entrepreneurs secrets
- make business through the Internet
- increase your popularity
- think big

A book that has the rare ability of **doing good to people who read it** (and if this doesn't mean being deeply *moral...*), by inciting creativity, inventiveness, the will to take practical measures and believe in your own ideas. And I'm not just speaking about *entrepreneur readers*: I'm not an entrepreneur, but **I found in this book a continuous incentive to improve my ideas in the artistic and literary field.** I conceived new ways to promote my products and, most of all, I learned to believe in them, in their commercialization and in their innovative potential.

Abate's writing **reminds to orality**, to direct and verbal communication: by reading his book you will have the concrete impression that the author's *talking to you.*

You will discover and take as example amazing but true stories of real entrepreneurs, such as **Steve Jobs**, Lamborghini, Grom; you will learn all the **web marketing** benefits, from *couponing* to *pay-per-click*; you will learn that it's never too soon to become an entrepreneur: **Jeff Bezos** and Jack Dorsey teach!

But, above all, you'll understand that "**nothing is revolutionary until it's created**", quoting the author.

In conclusion: **if a book to become rich, wishful thinker, resourceful exists...** ***it's this one.***

Daniele Corradi
H. E. at HOW2 Publishing

Introduction: The box of wishes

Why did I write this book? And who am I to write this book? **I'm a dreamer.** Someone who believes in dreams. I think there's no dream that can't come true and there's nothing better than realize a wish, believe in yourself and in your dream, selling it to other people who will share it with you and will help you realizing it.

But, my friend, nothing is easy, I'm not selling you smoke. To make dreams come true you'll need effort and perseverance, ideas and intuition. But, most of all, it's important to believe in yourself and your own ideas, against everyone and everything.

Starting from scratch, in these years, **I gave job to hundreds of people**, put into contact people I don't even know. But, above all, **every day I share my dream with people who believe in me** and in the work we, together, carry on with faith and passion.

When you have an idea or a dream, a wish, don't find right away an alibi for not realizing it. Let go the "it exists already", the "there's a crisis", the "it won't work". Don't let opinions and suggestions of other people condition you. It's your dream and you must protect it tooth and nail, as your son. It's all up to you and remember that what matters most it's not the idea itself, but the way you realize it, because nothing is impossible. Think always big and act without biting off more than you can chew, with strategy, vision and certainty.

If you have a secret wish, and I know you do, you **MUST realize it right now**, because our time is limited and wishes have to be realized, otherwise they will remain dreams for ever.

In this book you'll find the key for your box of wishes. It's there, waiting for you, at the very bottom of this book.

So, what are you waiting for? Break a leg, my friend. You'll make it.

Dario Abate

1. ARE YOU BORN ENTREPRENEUR? FIND IT OUT RIGHT NOW!

1.1. The essential qualities of a successful entrepreneur

Let's start from some questions. Are entrepreneurs born or made? And what's the difference between a successful and an ordinary entrepreneur? Who really becomes a successful entrepreneur is endowed with **talent** and **vocation** that manages to express and realize naturally. Let's take the example of the soccer player that hits the big time and becomes famous. He plays in the national team and even wins a World Cup. Lots of children begin play soccer because they're pushed from their parents who transfer on their child their own dream: became a successful soccer player. These children will never become big, because it's not automatic that they're gifted or have the will of becoming pro; they simply try because pushed by someone else's will. This approach is completely wrong, because the first rule to have success is **having the will to reach your own goals,** not someone else's, or doing something just to please others. Therefore, the first rule of the aspiring successful entrepreneur is to want it. And he must find inside himself great **aspiration, ambitions** and **will to succeed.**

There are many cases of sons of great entrepreneurs who had inherit a giant business, but had squandered it going bankrupt and making thousands of employees lose their jobs. All of this because they weren't **entrepreneurs inside,** they didn't want to be entrepreneurs in their lives; maybe they dreamed to be musicians or they would live a simple and stressless life, as any ordinary man. Basically, they didn't have this ambition, this will, this goal and this **determination.** So, dear reader, are you absolutely sure of becoming an entrepreneur despite all the difficulties and responsibilities you must bear? Since you were a child, all you do is **dreaming** of being an entrepreneur? Are you actually endowed with an irrepressible ambition of becoming a successful entrepreneur? If these premise and this will are missing, you'll never become a successful entrepreneur. Getting back to the sportive example, if you have talent and vocation but you don't have determination, **abnegation** and **backbone,** only the talent won't be enough to reach your goal. This is true in sport but also, in general, in life. History is full of examples of young, very gifted soccer players who could become very big, but that, without determination and **inner strength** failed and they never have become *someone.* Let's mention the example of **the French, world champion, soccer player Thierry Henry**, who told of knowing, in the early days of his sporting career, players with a talent way better than his own, but who get lost on the way since they didn't have backbone and willpower. They get distracted by youth temptations or gave up at the first obstacle, ending up doing waiters or bartenders for all their life. Henry, instead, thanks to his great **vocation**, his great willpower and abnegation became a world champion, despite having common technical means.

Therefore, **entrepreneurial talent is not enough if it's not well-supported** by an appropriate willpower, **spirit of sacrifice** and abnegation, in other words, by ***backbone***. So, let's add a second factor, besides vocation: the big entrepreneur needs "**balls**", I mean, an innate willpower, since the self-made entrepreneur career is full of great difficulties. The difference between the losing entrepreneur, designed for failure, and the winning one, designed for success and for earning lots of money, is, besides vocation, a **fighting spirit,** the **determination** of overcoming obstacles and knowing how to get over a failure.

1.2. Never be afraid of failing

Let's be clear, failure is a central topic in business. Entrepreneur must fear failure but he absolutely must not *be afraid* of it: he must not live it as a nightmare, but more as something that will help him doing his best. You have to **respect the fear of failing**, which must be seen as a great **inner motivation**, and always in **constructive terms**, even in the unlucky event of actual failure. Let's quote the example of the great entrepreneur and best seller writer Robert Kiyosaki, who claims that failure is part of an entrepreneur life and every entrepreneur is designed for failing at least once in life. Failure is a great school that even the number one amongst entrepreneurs, at least once in life, has to face. So failure must be seen as something that helps the entrepreneur to grow up, because **you learn from your mistakes.** But entrepreneur strength is learning lessons from failures and knowing to get back on his feet; he must treasure the mistakes he made and led him to failure, not repeat the same missteps and do always better.

Think about **the child when learns to walk**. As far as I know, a child who learns to walk falls at least once or a kid who learns to ride a bike tumbles down grazing himself maybe more than once. And, similarly, any newly-qualified driver did at least one little car accident because of inexperience (never scratch the bumper, you say? Good for you!). It's true, though that in some cases you really can't make a mistake, as in the case of the parachutist. If he makes a mistake, he probably wouldn't have another chance. In that case you can only rely on a very meticulous control of every variable and on a almost infallible preparation, that, I'm afraid, sadly doesn't exist. It's proven by many parachutist that every year, due to a fatal error, die. But **for the entrepreneur infallibility doesn't exist,** because he has to deal with too many variables. Of course, the more he has preparation, intuition and skill, the less he has chance to fail. But, in a real business, there will always be a chance to fail.

A successful entrepreneur must be **critical, analytical,** he must **understand his own mistakes** and, from failure, he must **get back on his feet** stronger and more determined than ever. I'm not saying that failure is an entrepreneur's friend or that he must fail sooner or later, but I'm just saying that failure is not the entrepreneur's grave and he must not be paralyzed by the fall fear. The momentary slip-up has to be lived just as a pause and the entrepreneur must live it in a constructive and positive way to go further and further, to **be stronger and stronger** and to **fly higher and higher**.

Is there someone who has never had a romantic setback? In the end, they are little personal failures. Do you change sex or retire to a cloister because of new romantic failures fear? Of course not. Instead you gain experience and treasure your own mistakes, trying again, until you find the right person. In business it works the same. It can happen to take the wrong business or field, but the important thing is not persevering in errors and having the strength and rapidity to change course.

1.3. The secret of "the sun in the pocket"

The successful entrepreneur must have another essential requisite, besides the yet told ones, which is an innate **inner positivity** and an innate **optimism**, that is "**the sun in the pocket**". Entrepreneur life is full of risks which, sometimes, don't produce damages; other times they can produce something negative. The important thing is **always overcoming obstacles**, treasuring your own mistakes and repeating them never again.

So, what's "the sun in the pocket" for a successful entrepreneur? It's optimism, which is that positive way to see life and business; it's the winning way in which we see things and opportunities around us. Optimism is that motivation which makes us seize opportunities even from something apparently negative; optimism leads us to **always find the good in all things.** Optimism is also that force which supports us in difficult moments and makes us not to lose clarity of thought, not even among a lot a stress or huge responsibilities.

By and large, positivity and optimism are natural talents, innate in our DNA, but they're aspects on which you can work, too.

Luckily, man is a rational being with the ability of working on his own limits and changing for the better his way of being and seeing things. Therefore, it must be clear that a successful entrepreneur can't be such a thing without having a **huge optimism** and a **contagious positivity.**

Up against the inevitable negative events that life prospects sooner or later, the entrepreneur knows how **not to lose heart**, and if he does it, it's only for a moment; then he gets up and is able to see, even in the ugliest things, positive elements from which drawing strength to continue.

In general, it's said that **the great entrepreneur stands out from moments of crises.** In good times everyone is good, but it's in difficult times that you can distinguish the *great* entrepreneur from any businessman. Actually, it's in time of economic crisis that the biggest entrepreneurs stand out. This is great, because the great entrepreneur manages taking positivity even from negative situations and transforming it into opportunity and wealth. Let's make a practical example. If in a country there's an economic crisis means that there's a high unemployment rate and few job opportunities. A fundamental law upon which the economy is based claims that the relationship between supply and demand arises and depends on the bargaining power. So basically, if there is a serious economic crisis, there is a high job demand which will reduce the bargaining power of workers, who, in order to find a job, will settle for a low salary. The successful entrepreneur seizes an immense opportunity of this crisis, which is to avail himself of workers with low or very low cost, compared to normal market conditions. This, **for an entrepreneur who gives jobs**, is a great business profit. So, while the losing entrepreneur, in a historical contingency marked by economic crisis, thinks it's not a good time to do business and investments and will postpone to who knows when the starting time, playing defense and being himself a crisis victim, the successful entrepreneur, on the other hand, will be able to **exploit the crisis**, seizing the positivity of the moment and realizing that it is the right time to invest; then raises and plays attack, being sure to exploit the significant benefits and plenty of opportunities. Basically, in times of crisis, ordinary entrepreneurs fail, the real ones get richer and richer. The difference is only in their heads and aptitudes.

And, **beyond the false morality**, ask yourself whether it is better an entrepreneur that starts a company, creating new jobs and hiring new staff, as wages may be low, or an entrepreneur who gives up at the very beginning, deciding that it's better not risk investing his own money, and therefore does not create *anything*, neither the company nor the new jobs.

1.4. Do not create an alibi, love the challenge

Fundamental rule: the successful entrepreneur must **never create an alibi.** Entrepreneur who creates alibis is done, is a loser. Alibi is only an excuse to not take action, not react, not fight and not aim to success. Another fundamental aspect to succeed is **entrepreneur's love for challenge** and **risk**, even though calculate. An entrepreneur who doesn't love challenge and risk is not a real entrepreneur and it's better off doing something else. Real entrepreneur is a poker o monopoly player: he sits at the table for the fun of playing, being sure of his means but without the victory certainty. Playing gives him **adrenaline** and lack of risk would not do make feel him a true entrepreneur. There are so many aspiring entrepreneurs, gifted with such ambition, but not with love or just the ability to withstand challenges and risks. These are entre-preneurs that can't **handle failure fear.** They always hide themselves behind their own alibis, that are reasoning that only evaluate business risks in negative, inhibitor and restraining terms, never in positive and full-of-opportunities terms. Therefore, unconsciously, these thoughts lead them to a negative mental loop, a vicious circle that will lead them only to not act or postpone it to infinity. These **losing entrepreneurs** obsess only over risk related aspects, highlighting the negativity that will lead them only to a business paralysis. This is a fatal outcome due to their own pessimism. An example can be convincing yourself that there is too much competition in a certain field or that a specific business already exists, etc... .

This way of thinking will lead them to never act, while the successful entrepreneur is a real **man of action without mental inhibitions.**

If you're not a real man of action and if you don't learn to **go behind your limits**, you'll never be a successful entrepreneur.

There are **aspiring entrepreneurs, well prepared from a theoretical and technical point of view,** who know every detail of their area of interest and are very well documented on how to run a business, but because they are afraid of "letting go" and failing, they **never cross the line** that will lead them to be really, operationally and actually real entrepreneurs. They will always be entrepreneurs in their dreams, like someone who learns all baseball rules without never playing for fear of making a bad impression.

1.5. Do not overthink, jump in!

Driven by curiosity and thrill of **diving off a 10-meters-high cliff,** a man climbs on the top of the cliff. However, once on the top, he starts to fear diving, think about the fear of emptiness, feel dizzy or just fear of getting hurt and so he *temporizes*, he waits a very long time, until he decides not diving anymore. He decides to go back and, in this way, he runs even greater risks of falling.

Another man **goes to disco willing to meet a woman.** Once arrived, he spends hours at the bar, drinking and observing girls in the club. He never gets the courage to speaks to one of them. He wants to chat up but can't find the courage because of his negative thoughts, insecurities and fears. *What I'm going to say? Am I good looking? Am I funny enough?* In the end, defeated by all of these questions and fears, he won't meet any woman and will return home alone, depressed and frustrated for not having met any girl and not having even tried.

Without that instinct, that contempt of danger and without the safety of his means, even the most handsome guy will never speak even with the ugliest girl, held back by his own fears, while the ugliest guy, who won't have all these mental limits, will meet the most beautiful girls and will get laid with zero problems. Therefore, the real entrepreneur has to be a **risk-loving**, but not a fearful or paranoid man and not a hopeless and pathological plotter. He must be able to **take the challenge** and **overcome his own limits** by learning how to **manage his own weaknesses** and to overcome them. But this doesn't mean that a successful entrepreneur must a wild nut or a kamikaze because, actually, he has to know exactly what he's up against and his risk must be calculated.

Be careful, though: risk evaluation will never lead you to an absolute certainty of success, because there can always be an unknown variable able to invalidate the project success.

Otherwise, business wouldn't be called "business". In the event of failure on the first attempt, the entrepreneur will learn to analyze the mistakes he has made and, on the second attempt, he will do something better, not repeating the mistakes he already has made.

When you play basket or soccer with friends, do you like playing in the stronger or weaker team? **The entrepreneur doesn't want an easy win**, because he loves challenges and overcome his limits, he wants to face an obstacle course because this is the game, although it may seem difficult. Who wants an easy win is not an entrepreneur, because being an entrepreneur will always bring you risks, the famous **business risks.**

1.6. Eat bread and wishes: how to become a wishful thinker entrepreneur

The successful entrepreneur is an **innovator** because innovation means making a difference and **making a difference pays off**. With innovation, however, you can never be sure in advance to meet all the market favors. You can do all the market research you want, but often these can also be misleading. They will never be 100% reliable, and you can never really tell for sure if yours is a successful business, especially in a completely innovative field. The one who can't handle this kind of stress in a positive way, loving the challenge and also being a bit visionary and very bold, will never succeed and will never be a real entrepreneur, but just a follower.

But, do you have to be **an inventor like Leonardo da Vinci** for being a successful entrepreneur? Of course not: you can also be successful by **making small improvements and innovations** in products and services that already exist, because, let's remember one important thing, the entrepreneur who puts a priori the limit that a product or service already exists and therefore that his idea won't work, is absolutely a loser, a failure. **You don't really believe that Google was the first search engine on the Internet, do you?** Absolutely not, it was born after Yahoo and many others, but it was simply the most innovative one. When it entered the market it became a leader thanks to the strength of its ideas. Do you believe that Facebook was the first social network and Mark Zuckerberg actually invented social networks? Absolutely not, very famous social networks existed already all over the world, such as MySpace. Imagine if Zuckerberg had set this limit, creating the alibi that his project wouldn't work because of the presence of similar projects on the market. Facebook would never be born. Do you think that Facebook is the ultimate social network and that any other could never beat it? If so, you can think that, but I believe that it's absolutely not true. This is just your constraining idea. Sure, Google+ was a flop, but only for its fault, not Facebook's. Same speech about Steve Jobs's Apple computers, who wasn't the first to invent an operating system nor a personal computer, but simply he produced an O.S. so commercial as it can be quickly spread throughout the world.

Therefore there are many **entrepreneurial success stimuli.** One of them is innovation. But **innovation can be absolute or incremental**, which means partial compared with something that already exists, but you manage to offer a new and better service than the previous one and the competition; an incremental innovation is able to achieve success on the market along with the ability to evolve, from *new entry* to number one in that specific area, or to upset the market itself. Perhaps, after Henry Ford invented the car, were other car manufacturers not born? Absolutely not! So, never set psychological limits thinking that something like your idea already exists and it won't work; rather think about how your idea is different compared with the others and how it can offer more to the customer, or it can enrich and improve a specific field, taking it to a new evolutive level.

1.7. Do not let others limit you

The successful entrepreneur always measure against other people, but he never lets them limit him. No one can scare him with inauspicious advice dictated by lack of vision, envy, or other negative factors. The successful entrepreneur can ask for advice and opinions to family, friends, colleagues or consultants, but in the end he decides with his own mind and, if he really loves and believes in **his project, he carries it on despite the negative opinion of all the others. Ferruccio Lamborghini**, before making super cars, was a simple tractor manufacturer. One day, wishing for himself a sport car with all mod cons, he commissioned one to Enzo Ferrari. He replied that his cars were only sport ones and not comfortable luxury cars, so he would never produce a car like that. Lamborghini then, as an act of defiance, decided to build himself a luxury sport car: thus the legend of Lamborghini was born. Do you think that, when he was about to take this bizarre decision, no one has laughed at him or thought he was crazy? How can a simple tractor manufacturer build a car more beautiful than a Ferrari? Objectively, this aspect is really amusing, but let's think what would happen if these negative opinions had stopped Mr. Lamborghini in following his idea. Lamborghini would never be born.

1.8. Bet all on yourself

The successful entrepreneur must **unconditionally believe in himself** and his ideas, love them even against the advice of others, even if the negative opinions come from people who love him. Entrepreneur must believe in himself and love his ideas and projects. He also needs to trust others, because there is no business that can be done only by yourself. There are sport feats you can do by yourself, but I have almost never seen businesses run by yourself. Be careful though, I'**m not saying you need a partner, but excellent consultants and employees.** One of the biggest mistakes new entrepreneurs make is getting in partnership with other people **for fear of acting on their own.** Business is like a body made of head, arms and legs. The head instantly coordinates the movements, but a two-headed body, before making a single movement, has to balance the two heads and if the two heads don't feel the same way, try to imagine the consequences. Of course, there are also many cases of successful businesses run by two businessmen partners, such as Dolce & Gabbana, but they are rare cases in which the two entrepreneurs are complementary or in perfect harmony. In many other cases, however, you look for a partner just because you want to share with someone your fears, thinking that in union there is strength. On the contrary, this choice might be a fatal mistake for the company life, as **all decisions should be timely** and if there isn't a complete ideas and intents sharing, this conflict can lead to company immobility or even to its death. Never make the mistake of looking for business partners only to overcome your fears: that would be a fatal mistake in the long run. As it's often said, the best company is the one with **only one partner.** The most precious thing for an entrepreneur, actually, is the **decision-making autonomy**, which means having **the power of the last word.** Just think of what it may mean having to discuss every single decision, facing, perhaps, exhausting debates. Do we realize what a waste of energy, what a stress and, in the long run, what kind of lethal consequences all of this can cause to the company? So, be very careful **not to share power**, because this is the biggest entrepreneur resource Surround yourself with good employees and consultants, but always maintain the authority of choosing and deciding, that is always maintain decision-making autonomy and operating power.

1.9. Visions strength: Steve Jobs

Qualities absolutely essential for a successful entrepreneur are **imagination, creativity and visionariness.** The most striking example of this is embodied in Steve Jobs. Do you really believe that Steve Jobs was a computer and electronics magician? Absolutely not! Jobs was just a mad visionary, who was famous for the sentence **"stay hungry, stay foolish"**. Jobs was just a guy with an insane creativity and visionariness, but he didn't know anything about computers and microchips. Driven by the force of his ideas and visions, he used the technical skills of his friend Steve Wozniak, who took delight in building small amateur computer at home, without any ambition of business. Without Jobs, Wozniak probably would have become a common and anonymous computer technician or, perhaps, would have completely changed profession and became a post office clerk. Instead, thanks to his friend Jobs, he became a billionaire. On the other hand, according to you, Jobs without Wozniak would become a god anyway? *Absolutely.* If Wozniac hadn't gone along with his friend, getting involved in ideas almost meaningless, surely Jobs would have continued without him, taking advantage of the ability of any other computer technician. So, what really matters for a great entrepreneur is not specific technical skills, but the ideas and willpower. Always remember one thing: **you can buy technical skills, not ideas.** The real successful entrepreneur is the one who knows how to **create ideas and visions**, while technical skills can be bought at low cost, in the labor market. Much later in life, when he returned head of Apple, after a time "out", Jobs decided to jump into the mobile phone industry. Now it seems easy to connect the name of Apple to the most successful phone in history, the iPhone, but when Jobs first had the idea to create it, it was probably considered crazy. Many managers and analysts have thought it was impossible to defeat a world leader such as Nokia, starting from scratch and with zero market share. On the contrary, Apple, thanks to the power of Jobs's ideas, his visionariness, his **courage** and **determination**, not only entered the mobile phone field, but it has even outperformed the global leader Nokia, becoming itself a world leader and absolute innovator in the industry. Again, Jobs didn't create an absolute innovation, he didn't invent the mobile phone, but he had the amazing visionary power to create a completely new product, which has revolutionized the industry and the consumers communication habits. If you lack a strong analytical sense and a strong **creative and visionary intuition**, don't be an entrepreneur, try with some other job. In other cases, Jobs not only has radically innovated an industry, but also he literally invented new areas, such as the tablet and the digital music player (iPod and iPad). So, the great millionaire entrepreneur is the one who knows how to **not limit himself** and has a **visionary power** definitely above average.

Never set a limit because something already exists; progress teaches that everything goes always ahead and gets better, starting from scratch or not. Think of those who laughed of Ford, thinking that it could never exist a horseless carriage. Ford invented it. And think of those who lived 100 years ago and, amazed, saw the first cars, simple engine-driven coaches. Seeing those amazing cars, almost magical, had an absolute evoking power at that time. But, what do you think? At that time, could those men imagine current cars? And how will be the cars of tomorrow? The great entrepreneur is the one who has the vision, can **look far ahead** and knows how to **read the future**. Imagining the future makes him even a **dreamer**, but his great strength, finally, is to be able to realize his own ideas and dreams, turning them into reality.

It's easy thinking about visionariness in a modern and futuristic industry as the electronics one, but is less easy thinking the same way in a very traditional industry such as food, for example. Do you think you could become a millionaire with homemade ice creams starting from scratch, not being in the field and not knowing anything about how to make an ice cream? This is the story of two young Italians, Mr **Martinetti and Grom.** One day Guido Martinetti, who works in the wine industry, has a vision: **he thinks about the best ice cream in the world.** He thinks that the best ice cream in the world is simply made of pure and natural ingredients, it's not chemical like industrially made ice creams. It's made as in the old times, only with natural ingredients: this idea is absolutely trivial and seems that it doesn't worth one euro, right? It would appear so, but the young Martinetti, starting from this banal idea, opened ice cream parlors all over the world, revolutionizing the ice cream industry and becoming a millionaire. Martinetti didn't have any cultural background on ice cream, but he was absolutely sure of his ideas, so he sought help in other people, a bit like Jobs did with Wozniak. Besides not knowing anything about ice cream, Martinetti didn't know anything either of economics and management, that is entrepreneurship. From these premises, it would seem that Martinetti couldn't achieve any kind of success. Instead, he told his idea to his friend Federico Grom, a simple manager. Thanks to the force of his idea and his charisma, he managed to convince his friend Grom and so they began to get an education on the ice cream and to design *their* best ice cream in the world. So, working hard, they began opening their first ice-cream parlor. With great enthusiasm and seriousness, they opened new ones and get having their own industrial building and ice-cream parlors all over the world, becoming millionaire at the age of thirty. This may sound like a fairy tale, but it's pure reality and it teaches us that **it doesn't matter the quality of the idea but your inner strength** and what you're willing to do to realize it. Do you think that in this business adventure everything has been all a bed of roses or easy for the two new entrepreneurs? Of course not, but, despite an apparently banal idea, thanks only to their incredible enthusiasm and their willpower, they achieved amazing results. Therefore, **don't ever set limits, always think big** and don't worry too much about the idea you are working on: it doesn't have to be the idea that will change the fate of the world or the idea of the century; it can be even a banal idea but with strong points which certainly lead to success, if supported by enthusiasm, willpower and business skills, as well as intuition and perseverance.

Thinking that an entrepreneur should have a great knowledge of his business subject matter is a great limit and mistake. Simply, the entrepreneur must be the master of the idea he wants to lead to success and, if there's a lack in technical knowledge, he should be able to get involved the right people who know how to technically implement the project. So, remember this other fundamental consideration: the successful entrepreneur is the one who, if he can't work alone, knows how to involve other people and **delegate operational work** to others. So he must have **intuition in selecting the right people** to work with. They must not betray him but will work hard to achieve the goals of which they are in charge. **The entrepreneur should not be afraid to delegate to others and should never make the mistake of wanting to do everything by himself**, thinking that no one can do it better than he does. Those who think like this are not good entrepreneurs but technicians or at most freelancers. But **what's the difference between a freelancer and an entrepreneur?** The freelancer is someone who commits his technical skills, talent and abilities to someone else, i.e. a customer to whom the freelancer sells all himself, his work, his talent and his ideas, as a kind of employee. In some way he is his customers' employee, to whom he gives his direct service, but he is actually an employee of himself. I'm not speaking about the category of freelance entrepreneurs, who can open associated practices with hundreds of employees. These are real entrepreneurs because they enlarged, they focused on the needs of their customers, delegating the operational work to subordinate people, that is their employees. I'm speaking instead about the little professional who, for fear of delegating the work to others, always does everything by himself and remains always *little*. The freelancer, in practice, is like he one who rides a bicycle: **when he stops riding the bike stops.** So what it will happen to him if, unfortunately, he will get ill? He will remain without an income. Instead, the entrepreneur is the one who is not afraid to delegate, and then is able to **create an organization** that can live without him. Therefore, don't set limits, decide **not to do everything on your own**, trust others and **delegate the operational work**, concentrate on developing ideas and making money. **Don't stick forever on a single business**, but keep constantly alive creativity: continue creating and designing no stop, as Jobs did, going from computer to MP3, to phones and tablet.

Another entrepreneur's quality is **cynicism.** The entrepreneur has to think **in order to make profits**, so he shouldn't be a sentimental but a smart person who knows how to take advantage of the slightest opportunity, as well as others' weaknesses. The entrepreneur who has too many scruples and regrets is a failed entrepreneur. I don't mean commit a crime, violate other people's rights or laws, but take advantage of every slightest possible opportunity without too much hesitation, as **Bill Gates** did when he copied the operating system invented by Jobs and became, thanks to a different marketing strategy, the world's leader in operating systems with the famous brand Microsoft Windows. In turn, Jobs had previously built its own operating system Mac OS inspired by the research work conducted by

Xerox. So, citing physics, **nothing is created and nothing is destroyed, everything is transformed.** This physics law is partly true also in business, let's think about it. Actually, nothing is invented from scratch, but everything comes from something and this is often the deeper meaning of the terms "progress" and "evolution." The first car was nothing more than a carriage having an internal combustion engine instead of horses. Mobile phone is nothing more than a wireless phone that you can carry around even at great distances. The tablet is nothing more than a kind of notebook, but much lighter and touchscreen. The MP3 media player is none other than the son of the CD Walkman.

The great entrepreneur is the one who has the vision and **imagines the future**, reflecting not on people current needs, but on **their future needs** and, therefore, he thinks about how to improve their consumption and their lives. This is the **sense of progress and evolution**; if you exercise and learn thinking in this way, you will become visionary entrepreneurs with an endless source of ideas to be realized, as new Da Vinci. Once sketched the business idea, you'll seek people technically able to realize it, making one step at a time and never biting off more than you can chew, which might make you fall. But if you fall because of inexperience or too much passion in realizing your project, remember that your strength will be to stand up again and start from where you have fallen. That's what a great entrepreneur does. If you remain traumatized for life and you'll forever be discouraged from your mistakes and your first failure, you will never become great entrepreneurs. Which is why you have to learn this secret: **what matters is not only the idea, but knowing how to realize it**, fighting with all your strengths and beyond. Don't think that you are the only one in the world who can have creative ideas, dear reader; there are lots of people who may have ideas even better than yours, but they don't have all the other necessary skills to realize them. Do you remember players who were more technically gifted than Henry? You, like Henry, have to bet on your ideas and turn them into reality.

1.10. The Think Big commandment

Another sacred commandment is the one of **Think Big**. Be aware that realizing a small or a large project is always hard; you might as well think big and work on a very ambitious project, with far greater economic and unlimited potentiality. As Berlusconi used to say when he was a young real estate entrepreneur, building a palace or building an entire town is the same thing after all, because a city is nothing but a repetition of X palaces, so might as well point to the city.

So **never set limits** to your project ambition or, more generally, to all your ambitions. Don't limit yourself, hence. If you have studied or started working in a particular field, remember that this shouldn't be a constraint for you or a limit on what you do or can do. You can easily do business in an area diametrically opposite or in an area you don't know about it, as demonstrated by Jobs or the above mentioned Martinetti.

1.11. In business the piece of paper doesn't matter

Another rule is not setting any limit dictated by your culture or your level of education. Many millionaire entre-preneurs and number one in the world haven't completed their studies; so **for being a great entrepreneur you don't necessarily need a degree**, but only the qualities described above. Steve Jobs, Bill Gates or Mark Zuckerberg never finished school. There are also many cases of semi-illiterate millionaire entrepreneurs. This is because, in the end, for a great entrepreneur **doesn't matter knowledge, as much as the know-how and knowing how to make people do what you need.** If you wanna be a great entrepreneur, **experience** rather than study. A great entre-preneur hasn't to be an omniscient polymath, rather he has to "make right people do" the technical parts.

Getting back to the original question, if a great entre-preneur is born or made, it is generally more likely to be born entrepreneurs. This is mainly because of an education system that produces technicians and employees but not entrepreneurs. **Entrepreneur is someone who undertakes and the sooner he undertakes the better.** The entre-preneur must have great practical spirit and you can't learn this from books but from life. You have to take a challenge and get your hands dirty: the entrepreneur school is a school made in the field. So, the final tip of this chapter is doing, no ifs, ands or buts. If you can summarize all these information and skills using them in the field, valuing them day by day and working constantly on your projects, it will be the very life to bring you to success.

We saw that one of the main secrets of entrepreneurial success is not setting limits on yourself. Let's see it with an example. Do you know **Silvio Berlusconi**? Before being the Italian prime minister, famous and controversial international politician, Berlusconi was a great entrepreneur who, starting from scratch, became the richest man in Italy and one of the richest men in the world. He began his entrepreneurial career in real estate, building, when he was less than 30, a whole city near Milan called *Milano due*. But he didn't do it as most of entrepreneurs would it, that is only following speculative criteria, building ugly and cheap houses; he, instead built a futuristic city, where pedestrians never cross cars. Berlusconi was not an engineer or an architect, he had just graduated from law school, but was able to have visionary ideas and engage good architects and urban planners.

After a huge success, which made him famous in Italy as a great real estate agent, most of the entrepreneurs in his place would continue on that road and would specialize in real estate. Berlusconi instead, having endowed the city with a cable TV system and **having thus created a neighborhood TV,** gets close almost by chance to the television industry, understanding its enormous economic potential in that historical moment, dictated by the fact that Rai, the Italian national television, held, until then, the monopoly on the national television advertising market. But it wasn't enough for him establishing a simple local television like so many others; in a short time instead he created the second giant Italian television, equal to state television, involving in his projects the best professionals to achieve excellence. Then he threw himself into politics and became the Prime Minister in Italy. This story teaches us that the great successful entrepreneur never sets limits, never obsess over one single area but he has visions and turns them into money, *lots of* money. This story is similar to the most popular worldwide story, starring the great **Richard Branson, head of Virgin.** He began with an underground record company, then created an airline company and now the first interplanetary travel company. This also shows that the visionary successful entrepreneur sets no limits, but is **a dreamer able to realize economically his dreams.** Do you think that Berlusconi knew something about television or Branson about flights? Absolutely not, but this was also their strength: the real entrepreneur doesn't care about doing business in the area he knows best because he studied in that area, or because it's the area under his jurisdiction; the important thing, I repeat, is being pushed by the force of your dreams and ideas and buying other people's skills. It's not important that you're graduated or specialized in something, but it's important that you believe in your ideas and have the strength to carry them out against all odds, even against errors and failings. Branson himself, before founding the Virgin, had seen failing his own publishing house and his underground magazine; Berlusconi himself, in the course of his career, tried making business in the large-scale retail trade but failed, he founded a television in France and then closed it. But these obstacles have not stopped him, nor his legal problems. When **Phil Knight, founder of**

Nike, began his entrepreneurial project, there was no other athletic shoe that Adidas, incomparable world leader. He hasn't started producing his own Nike shoes, but he began importing from Japan cheaper Onitsuka Tiger, and then started producing his own shoes as outsider. Not being able to compete economically with the advertising means of Adidas, his stroke of genius was to use as testimonial the transgressive image of some emerging athletes, loved by the public because different from others. So his motto was *"just do it"*. But do what? Inventing not the champion shoe, but the common people shoe, finding way into the heart of millions of aspiring, professional and amateur athletes. **People love heroic stories like the one of David and Goliath,** where the weaker can defeat the stronger, despite everything may seem against him. Which why people sympathize with the weak, with the "little but with personality"; the charisma of a different and strong brand is a winning strategy to aspire to fight and win, even against the strongest that seem unbeatable. Don't be afraid of anything and anyone, just believe in what you do and fight until the end, until every ounce of your strength. Don't feel frustrated if you are little in the beginning and remember that you climb the ladder one step at a time, the important thing is not to fall..Remember that **being small** is not a disadvantage but a great strength, because it **allows us to make quick choices** and quick changes about our strategies, while the big giants are restricted as pachyderms, which move very slowly. So, let's beat them on speed, flexibility and innovation.

Secrets revealed in this chapter

- First rule for success is having the will to achieve your own goals, not others'.
- Entrepreneurial talent is not enough if it's not well-supported by spirit of sacrifice and abnegation, in other words, by *backbone*.
- For the entrepreneur there's not such a thing as infallibility: don't be afraid of failure.
- The successful entrepreneur has an overflowing optimism and a contagious positivity.
- The real entrepreneur loves challenge and risk.
- Theoretical and technical preparation is not worth as much as the visionary power of your dreams.
- Innovation can be incremental or absolute: you can improve an idea that already exists.
- The decision-making autonomy is crucial to the successful entrepreneur: you do not need partners!
- Entrepreneur should not be afraid to delegate technical tasks to trained employees.
- Never set limits.

2. THE ENTREPRENEUR MIND

2.1. Think you must know before starting: the entrepreneur is just one

In the previous chapter we analyzed the inner qualities that an entrepreneur must have to succeed. If you have read carefully the first chapter, try to re-read it now and then think about it, make a self-examination to figure out **which of the described qualities you already have** and what you have to work on instead. Do it before reading the second chapter and move forward in reading the book.

Done? Okay, let's go on.

In this second chapter, before thinking about business, about what to do and not to do and how to do it, let's think about some things that you absolutely need to know before starting. First of all, some believe that there are different types of entrepreneurs, but I think **the successful entrepreneur is only one, and satisfies the requirements described in the first chapter.** Entrepreneur is someone who takes something from scratch and aims directly to success. So, let's clarify something: **who inherits a family business that he hasn't established is not an entrepreneur but is at most a manager**; if he is good, he will contribute to the company growth and will be able to develop new products, services, enter new markets and increase the sales volume... but how a good external, hired manager would do. For this reason, he isn't an entrepreneur only because he's the owner, but he's the owner and manager of a company that his father (or whoever), as an *entrepreneur*, has founded. However, if this person, although working in the family business, founded another, completely different company **from scratch,** then he can be defined a true entrepreneur.

The true entrepreneur is the one who has a business idea, that as a seed sows and waters, making a sprig grow, day by day, until this sprig becomes ***a plant***, a tree that bears fruit and will germinate other plants. The speed with which the entrepreneur can reap the benefits of his company depends on the quality of the plant and on his skill in making it grow; so this can happen soon, late, or even *never*, if the plant is dried before the due time.

Another similarity that can be done is the one with **a new dad.** Founding a company is like giving birth to a son and become father. At first, the child will need all our care and attention, because he isn't independent and old enough, so we have to take great care to make him grow well, to make that anything wrong doesn't happen and to educate him. We will make any kind of choice for him and will always be close until he grows up and is independent. The way is long: he will begin to crawl, then to take the first very insecure steps before starting to walk properly on his legs, on his own, and finally running like a champ. Same thing happens when we create a company, and then **we give birth to a new business.** We wouldn't dream of abandoning to himself before its time, right? We do, instead, all that is in our power, and sometimes even more, to make sure that everything will be fine, that the odds will be in his favor, that he will have the right means to walk straight and secure.

2.2. Why do you want to be an entrepreneur?

Before starting working on your business project, ask yourself this important question: **why am I doing this?** If your answer is "I do it because I can't find a job and I have to make something up and that's why I become entrepreneur", you are on a bad road. **It's impossible being an entrepreneur to have a job**: you would be destined for certain failure. You can be an entrepreneur only as a vocation, having in your heart a feeling like a religion, the so-called *fire inside.* Being an entrepreneur is something born from a passion and a dream you want realize; the guiding principle is the one of "you have it or you don't". Often you start a freelance job and you declare yourself an entre-preneur, but actually you're a simply freelancer. **The success-sful entrepreneur has dreams in his mind**, big and ambitious projects to realize; he doesn't simply need a job. If you just need a job, don't take into consideration the opportunity to run your own business as entrepreneurs, but just be patient until you find one. Instead, if you feel that fire inside and that vocation and you have big secret wishes, great inner strength to overcome all obstacles that separate you from their realization, then you can head off on this adventure. But **what's the difference between a little entrepreneur and a great one** designed for success and greatness? The little entrepreneur lives and-to-mouth and works to bring home a paycheck; he just does it as a freelancer, without having a boss and being the owner of his own initiative and business. He has no ambition to create new jobs and build an empire, or something that will grow more and more; he thinks only in terms of monthly earnings. So, he doesn't make some investment in order to have bigger gains tomorrow; he thinks instead of just save that money today. So he has a myopic very limited view of things; **his gazes is oriented towards the floor, not towards the horizon.** If you want to be entrepreneurs only to pay mortgage and bills and get to the end of the month with a salary, don't even try doing it: you'll fail. You're too close-minded to be able to define yourself an entrepreneur. At most, open a shop and become a shop keeper.

The entrepreneur, on the contrary, doesn't plan to open a shop and earn only from that store, but he **already sees a *national, or even international, franchising*,** because he only thinks big; so he starts with one step at a time by opening the first store, but he already knows that this is the pilot store for a great and famous worldwide franchising.

Ambition test. If you open a store, do you think of the its success and maximizing your earnings to take home the most money at the end of the month, or rather put all the money aside because you think of when you'll open the second one, the third one, the fourth one and all the other stores, becoming the owner of a chain?

Don't give me a granted answer only to deceive yourself, because between the two of them there's a huge difference. **Are you willing to risk? Are you willing to test your ideas** (and I mean a global test), or do you want to play it safe, redoing something that has already succeed? If you don't even want to think about all these issues, but **you**

simply want to run your shop without worries, your business will be like millions of others around the world, and I only recommend you to open it in a good position, to choose a good commercial location: avoid opening it in a street with little traffic, at least think about this. Then look after your store and keep it always clean and in good order, so that it will be a nice place to visit. Finally, you must have a very jovial and smiling attitude with your customers; if you're a bear, you're doomed to failure. An alternative: make sure that customers are handled by someone more cheerful than you. So, if you follow these recommendations is fine, open up your shop and good luck, but don't you dare to call yourself, now or ever, a great successful entrepreneur, even if your store goes well. If that happens, you'll put a lot of money aside, you'll buy a nice house and a nice car and you'll make a great holiday around the world... but I repeat: don't ever pass yourself as a great entrepreneur.

But if all this makes you sick and you're not satisfied, but you have much higher ambitions... well, on paper, you can become a great entrepreneur destined for success. But in this second case, prepare well all the details of the dream you want realize. We said that you don't want build only a store, but you want that this store in the future, will be the first of a large worldwide chain of similar stores. Therefore, **design the image and your services delivery so that it is standardized and replicable at low cost anywhere.** Think that what works in your city has to work on the other side of the world... Think well on this. **Don't think only about what you or your friends like** or what people who live in your city or in your country like, but think whether this thing, this idea, this new product can also be liked in other nations of your continent and other continents as well. Don't rely on other people advice, even if they're good, but act only with your head, gathering information on the Internet and in the field. In the end, **despite all the researches, make the decisions that you believe appropriate, based on your reasoning and your instincts.** You must be the only responsible and creator of your own destiny, no one else can decide for yourself; if you don't have this inner strength, forget it, entrepreneurship is not your thing.

2.3. Tipped for success

Another question I ask you to see if you're meant to be an entrepreneur is whether you're tipped for success. Are you willing to give all yourself to realize your project, sacrificing everything else, that is all your time, social relationships, your hobbies and your family? Your relationship with **your future business is like a marriage**: you have to love and respect it every moment of your life, be faithful, you must never betray it, you have to respect it aways, for better or for worse, by remaining always close to it. Are you willing to do all of this? Think about it. Are you willing to make economic and not sacrifices to make your business grow in times of need, and continually investing in it for its growth? That is to say, a bird in the hand is worth two in the bush? **Are you willing to leave your partner go if she throws you a spanner in the works, because she will say that you ignore her to take too much care of your business and your work?** If the answer to all these questions is always yes, I think you're okay.

Remember: if you decide to be an entrepreneur, **no one will ever do you any job interview,** as if you were to be hired in a company, so you must do the selection on your own: it's a self-selection and only you can tell if you can do it or not. So learn how to do an interview with yourself and, if you have to, make your own selection.

The successful entrepreneur must have an innate courage and innate inner strength, but that doesn't mean he can underestimate difficulties and obstacles or be irresponsible and reckless; the entrepreneur, like a good boxer, should know that, going **on the business ring**, he can give but also take punches. If you are aware of all of this and all of this doesn't scare you off, but rather excites you because you love the challenge, this is definitely a good assumption. Remember: **entrepreneur is not a job but a way of being**, a way of life and a mission.

2.4. Make love with your idea

Dear aspiring successful entrepreneur, I hope you recognize yourself in all the words read so far, but I have other questions to ask you. Let's start right now.

Basically do you tend to have business ideas related to your background or your field, or do you have **any business idea, even random, based on spontaneous ideas that you may have had looking at facts and things of life and the world?** If you see yourself more in the first case you are a bit limited as entrepreneur, because, in my opinion, the successful entrepreneur doesn't have to set limits, and if he gets an idea about some service he's not familiar with, this shouldn't be a problem for him, he doesn't have to put the idea aside just because he doesn't know deeply that particular thing or field. **A truly successful entrepreneur is the one who has brilliant ideas regardless the kind of service** or sector, although initially he is completely in the dark and far from that area; the problem, ultimately, is not the technical part or who will technically implement this or that part, but it's getting to have the vision. The important thing for the successful entrepreneur is **having the vision**; regarding the resolution of technical and operational problems, it will be developed by who knows about those specific fields, not directly by the entrepreneur. If you don't think like this, think well, because a closed-minded attitude will surely limit your way to success. It means you reason from a too technical standpoint and let technical aspects of things set your limits: there was never a thing wronger than this for an entrepreneur. It means that you have a technical-mathematical mindset, but that, for the successful entrepreneur, it's not basically a good thing or a plus, **because you overthink about the detail, but your mindset needs to be more open and creative.** Remember the example of Steve Jobs's Apple computers and Steve Wozniak. The latter was the mathematician, technician and the operative; Jobs was the mastermind, the visionary, the crazy guy. Do you feel more Wozniak or Jobs? Jobs greatness is that he had revolutionary and crazy ideas, but he didn't set limits, "the problem of how to do them", because he knew that it wouldn't be him to design them technically, but technicians hired for this purpose. So please, don't absolutely set technical limits and limits in general. **When you have an idea**, get carried away by it, **make love to it**, develop it without thinking about everything that comes next, don't let your feelings influence you negatively, think positive, think big and just think of **how this idea will lead you to the glory.** Everything else comes later.

2.5. Entrepreneur culture: the doctor from Harvard and the ragamuffin

So far we have talked about the character perspective of the entrepreneur tipped for success and glory, but now let's also think of another aspect rather controversial, which is **his degree of education and training.** Well, according to you, with the same intelligence and capabilities, between a doctor graduated from Harvard and a person who doesn't have even a high school diploma, who is favorite to succeed? The answer is not so obvious. Let's say it depends. The doctor from Harvard may have a high level and qualification of a lot of skills and technical knowledge. The ragamuffin, however, won't definitely have enormous theoretical knowledge and skills, but he will have a great practicality, ability to adapt and maybe instinct. **Take a lion raised in captivity in a zoo** and suddenly put him into the savannah; do you think he can survive? Likely he'll starve or will be devoured by another predator stronger than him. This is the case of the doctor from Harvard. Until his graduation, what experiences and what jobs did he do? Has he ever actually worked? **Does he know what it really means being in the work world** or did he just read about it in books? Probably he would be perfect to be hired in a very big corporation and to be formed as a future top manager; but if he starts a business, despite all his theoretical knowledge, **life would probably tears him to pieces.**

On the other hand, if the ragamuffin was placed in a context such as a corporation, he may not stand two days (likely he would lack the political skills to make a career, the formal courtesies and strategic capabilities to conduct progressive advances in rank, to tighten alliances with colleagues and get in the right light with the important top managers), but if he was asked to make money on the street, he probably succeed much better than the guy from Harvard, because he has **already learned** how hard life is, what it really means to live among people; he began working before, has been through all sorts of things and **knows what it means to make a living**. With same level of intelligence and creativity, the ragamuffin, probably for his ability of doing with what he's got and his strong resistance to negative phenomena, to the unexpected, to his ability to adapt and flexibility, might have even more chance of success than the brain from Harvard, who grew up in a golden cage. I don't want to be racist against anyone who has reached a great level of skills and qualifications and a high-profile school education, but simply I invite you to think again about the fact that many of the biggest billionaires in the world don't have a great educational background, and very often they are not even graduated. Many of them, who had a great entrepreneurial fire in their hearts, have started their own business adventure before graduating and the boom they made prematurely led them to not have enough time to finish school... but at that point, it didn't matter so much. So, don't hide behind **your pieces of paper because in real life they don't matter**; if you want to be entrepreneurs, no one will give you credit, you have to conquer all by yourself and you can frame that piece of paper and put it in the basement. **Generally, schools don't**

shape entrepreneurial mind and mindset, but soldiers suitable for being employees and doing their homework at best. **No one will teach you to be an entrepreneur: you will find out for yourself what it means** and how to do it at your best, as if you were thrown into the sea without knowing how to swim: either survive or drown. No one will throw you a life vest, so you are on your own. I hope that this book will give you many tips and useful ideas, but honestly (like the hundreds of books I have read on this subject) it cannot teach you being an entrepreneur *in your way*: you still have to learn this by yourself on the field, putting yourself on the line and starting to take one step at a time.

But getting back to us and to educational training, be careful: I don't want to diminish the importance of education, on the contrary; training and skills that you will make studying are important. I just want to say that they are not enough to be successful entrepreneurs. While you may have success by having the attributes, ie the "balls", but having little education, **you cannot succeed by having a lot of training, but few "balls".** So the message is this: you big doctors be humble and don't underestimate difficulties, even in the simplest tasks, don't take anything for granted because life is a little different from what you have read in your books; rather you humble people believe in yourself and don't be "neurotic" for not having that piece of paper, you're not inferior to anyone. **Success doesn't come from a piece of paper, but from ideas, from sweat and toil.**

2.6. How to conquer the world

Another very important tip: have always a clear idea of your goal and be always motivated by the desire to conquer the world, but remember that **you can't win the world in a day,** but day by day and you go up the ladder one step at a time; if you try to climb it more quickly, you might fall tumbling to the ground. Let's say that you've never swam because you can't swim. But no one can teach you, because, unfortunately, no one can swim around you. So you buy an on-line video lesson to learn how to swim and memorize all the theory. You have a lot of guts and look forward to begin testing what you've learned; so you go to the lake or to the sea. What do you do now? Do you have so much courage and self confidence as **to get on a boat, shove off and diving, or do you begin swimming onshore**, where you touch the ground? If your answer is the first one, I appreciate very much your bravery and your courage, but be aware that this can take you to make fatal choices and even to fail in your business. This is an extreme example in which your failure matches with your own death, while in business the result of your mistakes can be fatal for the life of your business... but not for your life. Be careful though, I don't mean that if you chose the first answer you are doomed to drown and fail, in fact you can also swim very well on the first try and even go across the lake by swimming or become world record holders in swimming at the Olympics .But be aware that **if your ego and your courage are boundless, you may run lots of risks**; you will probably be fine, but you would also have a lot better chances of failing. In this unfortunate event, I hope that your courage is at least equal to the strength of your reaction, your getting back on your feet and your moving on, without making the same mistakes of the past. If you have answered by choosing the second option (start swimming close to shore), you're people with common sense, with a lower risk of experiencing failure. Remember: **for an entrepreneur to be successful, he must surely be bold, but he doesn't have to be a fool**, a reckless kamikaze who can jeopardize every day the good things he built with hard work so far. If you are a poker player and you have a full house, do you gamble all your money in one hand or do you make a strong bet but keeping some money anyway, in case you lose that hand? And what do you do if you have a four of a kind of 10? My advice is always to keep away a bit of money, **unless you have four aces or a royal flush.** So, before starting with a business, ask yourself if you are ready and start to seriously look into yourself: you should definitely know that business success depends on the **entrepreneur mindset.** Once you've get your education in the field, as said above, **be always self confident and believe in your ideas,** stand up against everyone and everything, never be afraid of not making it and control your fears. Don't be afraid of not having enough *know-how,* that you can always gain; rather reflect whether you have the qualities of the entrepreneur or not. If you have only a few of them, try to figure out if you can work on yourself to improve your limits and overcome them, or, if you think that a particular aspect of your character doesn't have much room for improvement, think of whether this may be a manageable limit or not in your career as a successful entrepreneur. But don't forget: **always thinks positive** and try to find the solution to every problem, but **never be too analytical;** always remember that the entrepreneur is a doer, not a laboratory analyst. Think always more and more big, without ever setting limits, and remember that **we have only one life** and our time is limited; so do organize yourself, plan everything in detail, but *act*, don't waste time in vain, *do.* If you fail, do it again, play more and more **the amazing game of life and business**, with most of your enthusiasm and your strengths, never give in facing any obstacle. Remember that, if you want, **you can become *anything*;** everything here that's possible, if you dream it, you can realize it. Never set limits: nothing is impossible, if you want, you can. Even becoming the president of your nation or the new Pope if you really want it, and if you are thinking about it, you're gifted with enough intelligence and ambition, so work hard on yourself to achieve your goal, day by day. Get inspired by great men, read their stories, their biographies, learn their secrets, learn how and from where they started, try to emulate them. Establish goals that represent challenges for you and try to fight against the clock to reach them. Remember that **history is full of men who, starting from scratch, reached the most unimaginable milestones**; such as Napoleon Bonaparte, who wasn't of noble birth and was from Corsica, he wasn't even born in the important France; but thanks to his courage, to his ambition and determination, he climbed all the positions to become not only King of France, but also the emperor of a boundless empire. Or think of the lesser-known **history of Maximinus Thrax**, who, as an ordinary soldier, not even born in the Italian soil, became none less than emperor of the Roman Empire. So, think always big, and get inspired by the greatest trying to be one of them. Ok?

Secrets revealed in this chapter

- The little entrepreneur looks at the floor, the great entrepreneur looks at the horizon.
- If you want to open a large franchising or produce your idea on a global scale, design the image and your services delivery so that it is standardized and replicable at low cost anywhere.
- When you design a new product, don't think only about your taste, but think if this idea may be liked by other people, countries, nations.
- No one will teach you to be an entrepreneur: you will learn at first hand what it means and how doing it at your best. This is called *education in field.*
- Success doesn't come from a piece of paper, but from ideas, from sweat and toil.
- You win the world day by day.
- The successful entrepreneur must surely be bold, but doesn't have to be fool.
- Be always self confident and believe in your ideas, stand up against everyone and everything.
- Never be too analytical; the entrepreneur is a doer, not an analyst.
- Get inspired by great men actions.
- If you want, you can.

3. STRAIGHT TO SUCCESS: LET'S PREPARE THE WISHES SUITCASE

3.1. Define your entrepreneurial project

Let's continue this journey, which brings us closer to the realization of our business dream. If in the first two chapters we talked about the successful entrepreneur, in this chapter we get closer to **define our business plan**, preparing our wishes suitcase and the path that will lead us to success. If you have carefully read the first two chapters, have been thinking about what the qualities that you must have to aim to success should be and think that you're ready to start this wonderful adventure, keep reading; otherwise, pause again to re-read and reflect on the first two chapters.

Ready and motivated? Good: in this chapter we will clarify **how and what kind of decisions you must take in order to create and carry on your project,** your business. The most difficult and delicate part of the story is when you **decide what project to pursue**, and then which business you create. You have to trust blindly in the business you'll establish and give all of yourself to it, body and soul; so think carefully, because you have to be 100% sure. It's kind of choosing your life partner, with whom you will marry and raise a family; of course you can always get divorced, but with unpleasant consequences, so it's better choosing well from the start and not make mistakes.

First thing to do is thinking about your **wishes suitcase.** In this suitcase we have to put all our dreams, which means all the goals we want to achieve in this fantastic journey called business. **Do we want to put wealth?** How much? What are your goals and your ambitions in economic terms? What are your aspirations in terms of annual sales volume, when your business is up and running, after the first few years of *startup*?**1 million dollars, 5 million dollars, 500 million dollars or more?** Don't underestimate this question, it's not a daydream, but it's about definition of your economic ambitions degree, on which it depends the kind of project that you have defined. If you settle, for example, for 1 million dollars as annual sales volume, we can imagine an activity on a national scale. If you set your sight on exceeding 500 million dollars, you have to think straight away on a global scale. Please note that it's not so obvious that you should aim for an international project; maybe your ambitions are not so much extended. However, **change the design of your business from very beginning** whether your goals are of one kind rather than the other. Please note: I'm not saying that you will reach your economic goal within a very short time; this is up to you, but know that success is achieved with great effort, hard work and sacrifice, as well as a lot of talent, so it's good that you define your ambitions straight away. And then go: **do your best to achieve your goals, once you have them very clear.**

3.2. How to increase your popularity

Moving on to the second thing to put in the wishes suitcase: **your popularity.**

Do you dreams, as well as to become rich, to become famous, that is, a cover top dog? It's obvious that, regardless of this answer, if you manage to create a company like Facebook, Apple or Amazon, even if you don't want to, you'll end up on covers anyway. But regardless of whether fame and popularity are important for you, think of a business that puts a lot of emphasis on the figure of its founder, a business that turns a lot around you, that enhances yourself. What kind of character do you have? Are you a charismatic person or are you a shy and introverted person? If you don't have ambitions of personal fame, but only economic purposes, then do not worry about this aspect, let's leave it out of the suitcase. **If, however, your visibility is important** because you dream of being famous and becoming a popular and recognized person, then let's pause a moment to reflect on this. To achieve this goal, **you'll need to make clear choices of marketing and communications, from the very beginning.** Regardless of the kind of business or industry, this will be a critical step. It doesn't matter if you will establish an enterprise of products or services, nor in what area you'll work. In any case, you will need to design a brand and a business communication that revolves around the image of its founder. I hope that, if you want to take this path, you are provided with a very strong ego, and that by nature you are a very communicative and interesting person. If you work in an industry addressed to the mass, such as the food service, it's good that you have a positive and smiling look. But if you want to operate in services and advice industry is good that you have a very reliable and respectable look. So in any case, **you have to build yourself an image as if you were a cartoon or a show character and build your own reputation.** After all, in this case it's as if *you were yourself the brand*, so the stronger your image, the stronger the brand of your company. This process occurs more easily in the **products** industry and in some kinds of services, but it's more difficult to put to use it in other branches such as those related to **training**, or professional services and consulting. In the latter cases, in fact, you can't invent a character from scratch, because what matters are the stories behind him, his background and his training, because **you sell your skills, not just your face.** But even in this case, if you start putting you at the forefront, focusing a lot on yourself, you can get very far. Therefore create your distinctive style of attire, such as always using casual or elegant, as you prefer. Do you know **Marchionne** from Fiat? He always appears with the same casual sweaters. *And do you think it's a coincidence?* It's not! That look can mean many things: a determined "I don't need to put on the tie for anyone," along with a veiled "I dress like the people who work", for example.

If you opt for **a casual look, choose colors that stand you out,** such as red or blue, and always dress with sweaters or shirts of that color so that your appearance is memorable and *chromatically characterized*. You will promote firsthand your products or services, publishing video on-line in which you present firsthand your company and your products, emphasizing the qualities and selling as a first step your face and your reputation; therefore if you make this choice, be very careful and move with caution, because in case of failure you will burn forever also your image and your face, like a singer who made a flop.

On the other hand, if **you aspire to fame but you don't think to have a very charismatic and communicative personality**, don't worry: the fame will arrive anyway, later, when your product or your services will become popular; at that point, you will become, as a consequence popular too as the owner and founder of the successful company. Therefore the popularity will come automatically because they'll come to interview you, and then you can talk on the radio and on television or see your picture published in magazines and newspapers. This happened, for example, to **Mark Zuckerberg**, who wasn't extremely communicative and charismatic, unlike Steve Jobs who really has always been a guru. I personally suggest you, regardless of your personality, to opt for the second way, that is to **focus first on your company success**; once you have achieved your company success you'll get also your personal fame. I tell you this because at that point **your celebrity** will be earned and **truly real**, but if you rely exclusively on building your reputation, it will probably seem not credible and maybe you won't be liked by many, because your strongly characterize character could not be pleasant to everyone. Then consider once again that if something doesn't go exactly for the better, your image will be burned forever and it will not be easy recover you on a character level; therefore focus on your business, it's a suggestion.

3.3. Philanthropist or Wall Street wolf?

Last question to fill as best you can your wishes suitcase: **do you have philanthropic ambitions or are you only interested in personal goals?** Do you want to become famous as a magnanimous person, a sort of benefactor of humanity, or are you just interested in making money? Do you want to give a job to many people or that aspect for you is completely irrelevant? Based on all these answers you will have more information in order to define the ideal profile of your company. There are, for example, **companies that are improving the quality of people's lives**, such as Skype. Think about how much it was hard to communicate at a distance from one continent to another, until a few years ago. If you are a young person, for example a twenty-year-old, maybe you don't realize how the world was before. Today, wherever you are, you can see and talk to a person real-time, and this is a fantastic achievement, even though nowadays it seems perfectly normal and expected. For this, don't we want to thank the Swedish entrepreneur and philanthropist Niklas Zennström? Probably this great entrepreneur has never been interested in his personal fame, but rather in the good that his company could have done to humanity; in fact, when we think of **Skype, we don't think of who have founded it**.

And what about the one who founded **Wikipedia**? Do we realize how much he contributed to the *progress* of humanity with this project? Just think about how he has contributed to the spread of knowledge and culture in the world. Before Wikipedia you had to have a very expensive paper encyclopedia, which however was not updated in real time as it happens on the Web with Wikipedia, and so after a few years it was practically scrap. For all of this don't we want to thank to the infinitely the great Jimmy Wales? But also in this case, his name is not among the most famous on the earth, despite he truly deserves it. Probably a philanthropist as he is, after all, despises the personal popularity. In either case, if you are interested in your personal celebrity, I suggest you to call your company after your own name, as is common in car manufacturer, for example; let's think of the Ferrari, founded by **Enzo Ferrari,** or, better yet, **Walt Disney.** However, if you have an unpronounceable last name and you aim to an international business, just avoid this second option!

Now we have defined the values that are important for the entrepreneur in terms of economic ambitions, ambitions related to our personal celebrity and our sense of philanthropy and love for the world, in other words, the degree of gratitude we want from the world for our work. Be careful: conclusions of this analysis are not trivial and obvious, but they are worthing of a proper reflection. Think, for example, that Wikipedia is not a project for profit, and its founder has done good to humanity not being interested in money. Walt Disney, however, has done a lot of good to humanity, making it happier and more sentimental, but he has also become an immortal icon and has earned a lot of money, becoming one of the richest men on earth. Considerations are up to you.

3.4. The entrepreneur *mantra*

At this stage, unless you already have secret wishes or specific projects, you're looking for **inspiration to build a business idea** and a possible business; we are slowly clearing our head, like a sculptor who works a block of rough marble, and slowly, thanks to the chisel, will create his masterpiece improving it more and more. So far we have done a great use of the term *project* and **the verb plan**. You must understand that **for an entrepreneur this verb is very, very important** as to become his *mantra*. At any time of his day and of his life, day and night, he will think about planning and about some projects to be realized. **Project**, after all, **is synonymous with business** in the sense that the business is a kind of economic project. The verb plan comes from the Latin "proicio", which means to *throw forward*. Every action of the entrepreneur is related to the concept of planning, which basically means *move forward,* study the set of your moves and actions in all their phases, before moving to the executive phase. Let's make a practical example. **A construction project, that is create a building, is committed to an engineer.** First, he will make a collection of information and data from your customer, he will try to understand what kind of building he will design. Then he'll check which are the limits and possibilities on which to base his project in terms of laws and regulations. Then he'll move to the phase which is wrongly thought as project: the creative part of drawing. I say "wrongly" because, if the project is to create a building, this part is just *a piece* of the whole project, but it is not *the* project. **The project is the union of all phases**. Finally, you will move to the executive phase: the realization of the building. Ultimately, the building will be peopled and then used. This process is metaphor-rically similar to starting a business in all its phases. In this case, you, as a **potential entrepreneur, are both the engineer and the customer**; so if you want to build a building, it's the building that represents your business. So, you must decide what kind of building you want to build. A house, a condo, an office building, a skyscraper or a mall? For each type corresponds a particular kind of business. Then you will move to the phase of information on regulations analysis. In this case, out of metaphor, **the entrepreneur must decide whether his product or service can work and then he has to study the laws and regulations governing that specific industry**, do a market survey. However, he must sticks to what is your ideal project as much as possible. Once defined these aspects and made the necessary checks, he will start with the phase of drawing and definition of every technical detail of the project. In other words, the entrepreneur will have to study every detail of his business, understanding how it will work, which roles and skills will help to move the project forward; then what kind of product and service he will sell and what are the professional positions he needs to take off. He will design his company logo and will define brand and communication, which means the company image and a personal marketing strategy to launch his product or his services on the market. Finally, he will think about how to distribute the products or how to give visibility to his own services, what kind of sales force use and how to make it works. All of these are the project details. Once all these aspects are clear, the engineer is ready to start with the project: coordinate the work and move to the executive phase. Finally, the apartments will be sold and peopled and this corresponds to the sale of products and services, once put on the market. We have described, through a metaphor, a design process that takes us from our conception of the project to its realization.

3.5. A concept work: products or services?

I want to put your attention on another word, that is the term "***concept***". In the jargon of design, *concept* is actually the concept which describes the DNA of our company or of our project. **The stronger and distinctive our concept, the stronger the image and soul of our company.** When we create a company idea, we put this idea into a series of elements that create our concept, which is nothing than a collector of all the elements that represent the strength and soul of our company. The stronger our company concept, the more successful the company will have. So **the company concept has to be very distinctive and full of personality**, because it has to differentiate ourselves from our competitors and put us on a higher level than them, or at least more convenient for the market. In concept, therefore, we describe our company in a nutshell, as if it were **a preface to a book**: the more attractive the preface, the more likely who read it purchases the text, because he finds it interesting or because he recognizes in the preface those elements that catalyze *his* interest. Without all this in mind, we are finally faced with a choice of sides, that is one of those crossroads at which it is not easy to make a decision. Well, do we want to start **a business of products or services?** In both cases, you can open infinite series of scenarios. The question above is valid, of course, if you don't already have a business idea you want realize. If, however, until now, you have no idea in your box, but you are simply looking for inspiration because you dream about becoming a successful entrepreneur, then okay: let's think together.

3.5.1. Companies of products: Nike's success secrets

Working in the industry of services or products are two things diametrically opposed. It's like **traveling by plane or train**, for example. Generally, working in the industry of products is, for a business *start-upper*, more complex than working in the industry of services; in fact, there are more variables to manage and control and more investments to support. In the **field of products** you generally speak of the *production chain*, that is that process that goes from production to marketing. This is a very complicated process, in which there are many variables that change depending on the commodities sector. For example, in the food industry the perishable nature of the products is a key variable to which is related the time factor. In other industrial sectors, for example related to mechanics or electronics, there are other key variables, such as the international security standards and everything related to patents. For obvious reasons, here we can't go into detail, because there are too many fields to be analyzed according to the different commodities sectors of the product category taken into consideration; in short, we can say only that **working with products has a complexity and difficulty degree much higher for a newborn entrepreneur, compared to the sector of services**. But beware, there are of course many shortcuts to reach your goals. If you are interested in the category of products, to encourage you and give you a right example, let's mention the case of **Phil Knight of Nike.** He, like all the greatest, started absolutely from scratch, like you. Of course he didn't start right away by producing his Nike shoe as you see it today, but he did a *different* path, or rather *divergent*, in the Latin sense of the word (from the verb *divertere*, separate from). Since, at the time, the sport shoe par excellence in the United States was only Adidas, which held the monopoly of the market, he decided to start importing from Japan a great shoe, very cheap: the Onitsuka Tiger. It was a good product and with a very competitive price; Knight was not only a great seller, but above all he was a great entrepreneur: by organizing indeed an excellent sales network, he has started to gain very well commercializing the Onitsuka Tiger in the USA. Then, thanks to the proceeds, he invested all on his exclusive project, and thus he launched the Nike running shoe. What are **Nike's success secrets**? The product quality or the brand strength? At the beginning, Knight focused more on the brand strength, on marketing and communication: he made design the Nike logo, that "comma" which is one of the strongest knots in the history of graphic design. But, for a so successful and amazing logo, how many millions of dollars do you think he shelled out? Not even a thousand dollars! It may seem incredible that a brand that is now worthing billions of dollars did cost so little, right? Yet it is so, because Knight made it draw by a young novice graphic designer: that was his first logo with a fee, so Knight got by very few dollars. The Nike logo was not even drawn in a professional studio, but **on the kitchen table of this young professional**. That's amazing, isn't it? Think of Nike with a different logo, perhaps it would never have been success... who knows. But a great logo, clearly, it's not everything. Lacking large advertising budgets unlike his opponents, and in particular Adidas, Knight gave his promotion to very discussed and charismatic athletes, hired as testimonials. His fortune was directly associated to the success and the personal lives of these athletes, so that in a short time, Nike became a very famous brand in the world. But all this, of course, is not enough, because if everything is based only on image and communication, sooner or later the dream will vanish, because fashions are temporary. Knight, instead, began to invest a lot in research, aiming to create innovative products for his own sector and expanding more and more his product lines, moving from running shoes to shoes for all other sports. With regard to innovation, just cite **the case of the Nike Air Jordan**, the first shoe in the world with a cushion of air above his sole. Honestly I can't tell if, from technical and sportive point of view the air cushion could give something more to basketball players, but certainly, in terms of marketing, it was a truly revolutionary product, which established the Nike brand all over the world. Nike is the proof that **technology and communication go always hand in hand on the road to success,** in fact the sport shoes Nike Air Jordan caused so much clamor, not only because of its technological skills, but most of all thanks to Michael Jordan's name, the greatest player basketball at the time, and perhaps in history. Associating your brand to an incredibly popular and winning character makes perceive our brand and our company as a leading company, which is absolutely good for sales and sales volume, that is, for your wealth. So, inspired by Knight, **at the beginning aimed at people with huge potential,** on which you can bet as rising stars, and **grow up with**

them; later, when you will be a *top dog*, associate your image to those who are already as big as you, the Michael Jordan of the day. But be very careful: all champions are, however, *men*, so they may also have unexpectedly decadent curves, as what happened to Tiger Woods, suddenly declined because of sex scandals that have taken him from riches to rags, in terms of popularity; or think of the tragic and the more recent case of South African champion Oscar Pistorius: is useless to comment on the image and economic damage suffered by the companies that he sponsored.

Another factor to keep in mind, if you are oriented to work in the sector of companies of product, is related to the **cost of production**, ie labor costs. Today the western industrialized countries suffer a lot of pressure and competition from products originating from Eastern countries, where labor costs are far lower. Labor cost and taxation in force in a country weigh so heavy on the final price of a product. Beyond the quality you can offer, **the price of a product is crucial to your success** in the market. If you'll have a price out of the market, the consumer will not care anything about where you produce your product, whether in the United States, Germany or Korea, but he will judge it on the **value-price-image ratio**. In addition, there is a fourth variable that will determine your success in the market, which is the **visibility** of your product. So if you have a high price and limited distribution, therefore a low visibility and a weak image, despite the quality of the product is at the top, you will be doomed to failure, or to a very small niche of buyers. Therefore, if you opt to work in the category of products, I always suggest to **lower your production costs, ie labor and raw materials**, because the possibility of holding the price is always important for a company, beyond the quality it offers. **If you live in a country where labor costs are high and the tax burden is high,** and you want to become a global successful entrepreneur in the sector of products, there are two things you can do: either aim at an incredible quality and a very strong imagine, such as the greatest Italian fashion brands, Gucci, Ferragamo, etc; or go to produce abroad, in countries where labor is cheap, such as Cambodia, Vietnam and Taiwan. After all, it's what did the same Knight of Nike, which has even been involved in major scandals of humanitarian nature, from which he did really struggle to recover, when it came to light that his soccer balls were produced by children in the third world literally *exploited*. Without discussing moral issues, consider just these typical aspects in the business world of products.

Another problem in the sector of products is the **unsold**. In the event of failure of a product, it remains unsold and this causes serious economic damage to the company, reaching in some cases to drag it towards bankruptcy. If, however, you're sure, aim without fears at a company of products, but I just recommend you to think big, **think of a strong product that can please as many people as possible**; think, ultimately, to a potential global market. Finally, **try to be as innovative as possible**, whether you operate in an industry with a high degree of innovation or in a more classic one; always look for something that will differentiate you from the competition and that can give **something extra to consumers.** Be careful, **innovation does not have to lie in the characteristics of the product, but you can also innovate in communication and marketing**, in distribution and kind of store that will sell your product. However, be innovative and stand out from the competition, have a strong and distinctive brand.

3.5.2. Companies of products: how to interpret people needs

If you want to work with products, try to have a brilliant idea, which means try to **interpret the people needs**, to have a vision of the future. Don't just do what everyone else is doing: it's useless for you to produce a mediocre product, or an already existing identical one, why someone should buy your product and not all the others similar? We work on a **mental heuristic process.**Is there something that people need and that does not exist? Definitely yes, because I don't want to believe that in 100 years from now there will be the same devices, the same objects that there are now; a number of inventions and innovations will come gradually, over time. So, instead of waiting for others to make these inventions, try to think for yourself: **what could be done to improve people's life?** You don't have inevitably to invent a new product; let's also think about how we can improve existing products, for example. Make a brainstorming session with a trusted person, or even by yourself; sit at your desk and write on a sheet a number of objects that you can think of... now think *how they can be improved.* I'm sure you'll have a brilliant idea; then describe it on paper, so as not to forget it, outline it in all its details and don't set limits to your imagination: think even of things currently impossible to achieve, so it's just a concept. Basically it's the same process that takes place in the car sector when they work on a new car. It starts with a concept car, which is **a dream car**, from which then the real car comes. Once you have defined in detail your concept, that is your ideal product, your dream (so *brilliant*, I hope!), **do not absolutely make the mistake of talking about it with others**, who can cut down to size your idea precisely because it's an innovative product, or maybe even revolutionary. Know that people tends to be reactionary, which means that they do not accept the changes positively. People are creatures of habit and therefore they don't like change, because it's hard to adapt, to learn something new. Chances are, if you will describe your ideas to other people, for one reason or another, they will tell you that it can't work or, worse, that it' a crap. This is why **Steve Jobs was absolutely contrary to market researches**, because he said they could inhibit his creativity, which was boundless as he was a true visionary. In the end, market surveys are carried out by consulting *ordinary people*, who are used to seeing things in an ordinary way. These surveys can be fine if we are talking about common products that interviewed people know and normally use; but when it comes to innovative products, it is possible that they give negative feedback as they are not used to a new way of doing or seeing things. Don't worry, though; believe in your project and move on.

I give you another piece of advice. **In the initial phase of your project, try to cut all not essential costs**, that don't constitute a directly productive investment for your business. Avoid expensive market researches or expensive legal advice, and remember the example of Phil Knight who made the Nike logo draw by an unknown graphic designer for a few dollars. Remember that all of the biggest companies in the world, the richest ones, even those in the top ten, started from scratch, such as Google which began in a garage or Apple itself, which began at Steve Wozniak's home, Steve Jobs's partner. Remember this motto: **big ideas and little steps.**

Talking of going right to your own way, without being influenced by the advice of others, I quote an example. **It was 2002 and I was attending the faculty of Industrial Design at Politecnico of Milan.** We attended a laboratory for *product design*, taught by some of the most famous Italian product designers. I remember that we were so many, and one of the professors said something memorable: **"The mobile phone that takes pictures is a crap**; the phone is meant to make phone calls and the camera is meant to take pictures." It's been just over 10 years and now the phone does everything, except the coffee. So, always think with your own head and don't trust the advice of anyone, not even alleged guru. Be your own guru.

3.5.3. Three kinds of entrepreneurs

Let's get back for a moment to the wishes suitcase, the magic tool to define your goals and trace the outline of your ideal business. If your primary objective is to **generate profit in a safe and fast way**, a criterion of choice might be to **opt for the newest business, one in a strong growth phase**. In this case, the secret to have a success as large as possible is being very fast in taking action and establishing a company. Let's make a practical example. Who sensed early the business of the **electronic cigarette**, believing in it and in its great economic potential, has made a great choice. If you have decided to make it big, the entrepreneur in question has planned the launch of the business maybe deciding to open a chain of stores specialized in selling electronic cigarettes, with his own highly evocative and with a great personality brand; then he designed the communication of his business and the commercial format of the store in a distinctive way; then he launched a franchise consultant network and opened a store network in the country, or even abroad. This is a **speculative business**, in the sense that the entrepreneur is not so much interested in the type of product, but simply he recognize a fast growing business and seize the moment. In this case the motto is "so, is the pot getting sweeter", as in poker. The secret of success, in these cases, is based around the concept of *carpe diem*: move ahead of the others, do it with the highest possible timing. In these cases, as we have moved with cynicism, so we have to pick the right moment to even *get out* of the business, before the speculative bubble bursts. This kind of business in fact has an expiration date, it is like a balloon that is inflated more and more, until it bursts; therefore the secret is moving as quickly as possible, take advantage of the boom and get out of the business before the bubble bursts. In this specific case, being a product completely new and not yet regulated by specific laws and health regulations, many customers are switching from regular cigarettes to electronic cigarettes, and therefore around this product it's generating a turnover of global dimensions. But think what will happen when the market begins to saturate, which means that many different stores and many companies will open, like mushrooms (and keep in mind that, according to recent statistics, many businesses that were born only to treat the electronic cigarette have already closed); think of when laws that limit its use will come out, for example by declaring illegal to smoke electronic cigarettes in public places, or if it will be discovered that even the electronic cigarette is harmful to the passive smoker. In such cases, the business will collapse, and those who have established a small empire of stores could face the danger of failing suddenly; **the secret of good entrepreneur is therefore not too grow fond too much of his business**, and let it go in time in case of necessity. As an entrepreneur must have a nose in rushing headlong into a fast growing business, so he must have noise in giving up a business which is about to fail, such as music or audiovisual media at blockbuster. **Blockbuster** has created an global empire around the rent of DVD movies, but when the phenomenon of digital files started to explode, the market has shrunk considerably, and the failure was so fast to destroy the entire Blockbuster empire in no time. So bottom line, the entrepreneur must have flair and instinct, basic skills both to start a business and to finish it before it's too late. However, entrepreneurs of the speculative kind are primarily interested in the economic aspect of the company. They overshadow the popularity aspect and they completely ignore the philanthropic one. On the other hand, if you are an entrepreneur who belongs to the category of those who crave fame and personal glory, those who want to do something positive for society and not only think about the money that your business must generate, I can give you more advice. In this case, in fact, it's not only about choosing a business just because we see a great economic potential, but we think in other terms. **The glorious entrepreneur**, in fact, wants to launch a product or service that can improve the society and people's life. In this case you generally have to **focus on innovation**, because, to improve people's life, you have to launch an innovative product or service that is better than existing ones. To do so you have to be absolutely *open mind*, you have to think outside the boxes, "think different" again citing Apple, you have to disconnect from the crowd. To do so you must have a strong personality, because, as we have seen, revolutionary people usually suffer several attacks by most people who are rather conservative, and want to defend the status quo. You have to give a damn about what others will say and think of you, you have to go straight on your way, sure of your own ideas, without asking for help and moral support to others because you will probably be disappointed, and this may undermine your self-esteem and the belief that you have in your project. Those who think in these terms are generally a sort of guru, a sort of charismatic leader, **an opinion leader, or someone who generates opinion and is not subjected to the opinions of others.** The guru, for Hindus, is an undisputed master, who leads the others in an almost supernatural way. For being this kind of entrepreneur I give you a tip: focus on a specific training, that is **try to interpret the social changes that are taking place** and to think about what are the new people's needs. Just think of the enormous potentiality that technology offers day after day, and of all the news that it produces all the time. Think of Steve Jobs when he designed the **iPod.** At that time there were already MP3 that people downloaded using software such as Napster on their computer, but still people walked around with bulky devices like the Sony Walkman, a portable CD player. Portable CD players not only had the disadvantage of being bulky and heavy, but consumed many alkaline batteries, with very limited autonomy. Think also of how it was bulky to carry around so many CDs. Everything now seems prehistoric times, but if it hadn't arrived a visionary like Steve Jobs who invented the iPod, that would probably still be present. The iPod is not only a device of very small dimensions, and therefore very light and suitable also to jogging, but it is also very environmentally friendly, since it does not use alkaline batteries that are highly polluting, and so it gives the consumer enormous benefits also in economic terms, since you can upload lots of songs and the battery can be easily charged at home, without having to buy them every time. Don't take anything for granted, but think of the business aspect of this project, of how it has revolutionized the music world, the people's habits and needs, their quality of life. In addition, this event also caused the crisis of areas related to the old music, such as CD manufacturers. But this is progress and that's the economy, as when we have moved from vinyl to CD, or from VHS to DVD. So, reflect on visionary entrepreneur imagine. **Steve Jobs did not invent the MP3**, but he simply designed and launched a device that could read MP3, that is music files that were running around everywhere. Everything that already exists seems trivial and obvious, but when it was conceived, built and launched on the market it's something magical and brilliant, that will change the lives of millions of people or at least it helps to get them better. Same thing happened with the invention of the tablet and the world of Apps. So there is no secret formula to become a visionary entrepreneur like Jobs; you just have to train yourself to sense the needs of people, and to understand how to improve their lives through new services or products that do not yet exist, or represent the evolution of something that already exists. Remember: **if you don't do it, someone else will do it in your place.** So, become interpreter of the change and learn to repeat the every day the exercise of thinking of how will the world of the future be. After all, the visionary entrepreneur is a kind of mad inventor.

So far we have identified **two categories of entrepreneurs: the speculative entrepreneur** who thinks only about his profit; **the visionary entrepreneur** who thinks to invent new products or services. Finally there is **the third category: the philanthropic entrepreneur.** This is probably the most romantic figure of entrepreneurship, as the philanthropic entrepreneur has only one purpose in life: doing something to improve the world and leave an almost heroic and glorious memory of himself, as the world owed him a kind of eternal gratitude. For him, the economic aspect comes later, but the important thing is to create something that improves people's lives and enrich humanity not in a material sense, but **immaterial**, such as cultural or health. It is true that **Facebook** has made **Mark Zuckerberg** one of the richest men in the world, but it is also true that it has given something great to humanity, allowing to put in contact a lot of people that were physically distant, as it has strengthened the concept of *hyper communicativeness* and *hyper connectivity*. Or think about **the political value of Twitter**, thanks to which revolutions broke out in different parts of the world. I hope I've given enough stimulation, suggestions and ideas to think about!

3.5.4. Companies of services: billionaires with Internet or the immaterial power

Let's end this chapter by analyzing what it means to start a business in **the sector of services**. Working in services clearly means not having to produce something material as a product, but **something immaterial**: a service, to be precise. **Amazon**, for example, offers the service of on line sales of books and other products. **Groupon** offers a *couponing* service, thanks to which people can buy products and services from partner companies at highly discounted prices. **Airbnb** has created a new hospitality industry, allowing individuals to rent their houses or portions of their houses.

The companies I mentioned are companies of on line services who invented new industries almost from scratch, or completely innovating them, creating a whole series of follower and clone business that try to emulate their success. But you, dear aspiring successful entrepreneur, don't try necessarily to emulate services invented by others; rather, try to invent new ones. Consider that imagination and creativity have no limits, and **try to be a visionary rather than a follower.** Sure, it's much more impressive inventing completely new and radically innovative business, but that doesn't mean that we can't innovate even remaining in line with existing businesses, as for Google that was not the first search engine, but simply the best ever. When it comes to the Internet, please, do not ever think, even remotely, that everything already exists and everything has already been invented, because there is nothing more absolutely false: in fact, the Internet is still in its beginning, because it is massively running for less than 30 years. **Think of the Internet in 20 or 30 years**; I know it's not easy, but it serves to give you an incentive to change the way you see things. Therefore try to invent something new: **there is an endless potential out there**, like when you had to colonize the Old West and cowboys rode on boundless and endless prairies. Think of that time and think of what America is today, with all its skyscrapers and its megalopolis. Just think about how cities change: they change from day to day, and they are in constant and endless evolution; therefore, everything is always changing, you just need to be an interpreter of your own time and try to play a leading role in the economy society... but try to be *smart* and do it *quickly*, because our time is limited.

Be careful: in the category of companies of service there is not only the **Internet,** but honestly Internet, nowadays, is the sector with the greatest potential and the most rapidly growing rate, so it offers all the conditions for becoming a millionaire entrepreneur starting from scratch, operating easily on a global scale and allowing entrepreneurs to become famous and rich in no time, as it happened to Mark Zuckerberg of Facebook, Jack Dorsey of Twitter, Andrew Mason of Groupon, not to mention Larry Page, founder of Google, all young and super billionaires.

Well, at this point, the third chapter is complete, you should think about it and prepare everything you need for your wishes suitcase.

Before you read the next chapter, in which I will give you more operative tips on how to start your startup business, you should **jot down some ideas of business**, so that you can read the next chapter with already an idea on how to start the business of your dreams. Good job.

Secrets revealed in this chapter

- Define your goals clearly before you start your own business.
- Be your own brand. Build your reputation right away.
- Focus on the success of your business: your reputation will be earned and real.
- Making projects is doing business.
- The stronger and distinctive your *concept*, the stronger the image and soul of your company.
- Technology and communication should always be combined to achieve success.
- At the beginning of your business, relies on testimonials of talent and grow with them.
- In the initial phase of your project, try to cut all the not essential costs.
- Try to be a visionary rather than a follower.
- Don't talk about your big ideas to others: you might just run the risk of being cut down to size.
- Big ideas, little steps.
- Interpret the society changes: if you don't do it, someone else will.
- The secret of a good entrepreneur is never growing too fond to your own business, and let it go in time in case of need.
- There's an endless potential out there...

4. HOW TO RUN A SUCCESSFUL STARTUP

If you came to this point in the book, I hope you've already assimilated very well all the concepts contained in the previous chapters. Through the chapters one and two you have thought about what are the essential qualities of a successful entrepreneur, and you have made a self evaluation; in chapter three, instead, I hope you've been able to reflect on what kind of business you intend to bet on. If you don't have yet a clear idea you should pause more on the first three chapters, and continue to think until you have a clear mind, until when you find the right motivation and some planning idea. Instead, if you're ready, let's go ahead with the **operational part of the book**, that is, with the chapter of practical advice **to get started with your business startup.**

It doesn't matter if you've decided to focus on a company of products or services; in this chapter I will give you practical advice and an overview of how to organize and run your business.

4.1. How to prepare your *business plan*

First, according to the theory, **before starting a business the entrepreneur must prepare a detailed *business plan.*** The business plan is a strategic document which describes in detail, from every point of view, the business project that you want to realize. It starts with a more descriptive part where you describe the company; then you tells what it will do, in what market it will work and what are its competitors. In addition, you describe the strengths of the company, called "**competitive advantages**", thanks to which the company should be successful on the market as holding supply factors that other companies don't have, or at least with respect to which they are lower. Always remember that the entrepreneur is a strategic animal, and doing business is a little as **playing Monopoly or Risiko**: you need to prepare a war strategy and put it into action, battle after battle, to reach victory and success. Your competitors are the enemies you must defeat, gaining market share up to the leadership. This is the *game of the market.* To win this game you need to possess war weapons stronger than your opponents ones. Of course you will not only a weapon, but a number of them; but you have to focus on only a few to win the war.

One of your weapons is the price. Generally, having low prices is a strong competition weapon.

Another fatal weapon is the **quality of your product,** that the more is different from those of other opponents, the more it will give you a competitive advantage over them.

To simplify the matter, let's say that you should generally choose one of these two weapons, then aim at the lowest price of the market or focus on a highly differentiating product. So you should have, in either case, the stronger weapon than all your opponents fro being the war winner. If you have both of these weapons, but at a mediocre level, you will be the doomed to fail. To achieve success, you have to be number one in the use of at least one of these two weapons; never stand in midstream. Leaving the strategic aspect of this topic, let's move on to the business plan topic.

In the first part of the business plan you must state what you want to do, describe it in detail, indicating its strengths and stating **why you think that what you want to do is faithed to be successful on the market.** Then you will have your personal market survey according to the products you have chosen, which means you'll **describe the state of the industry and of the competition,** showing which are the weak points from which you will derive, for differentiation, strength and competitive advantage. The **analysis of competitors** is very important, because you have to know the smallest detail of your rivals, knowing perfectly their strengths and weaknesses; on those basis you will adapt your strategy of attack and defense. As you see, the business plan is like a battle plan and **you are the general who will lead the armies to victory or death.**

Once you have examined in detail your business and your competitors, you switch to the descriptive part of **how it will work technically your company.** In this part you will describe by whom and how your company is composed of and what functions and what resources it needs, both in human and in material terms. So it comes to company organization and logistics. **Business organization** means the **organizational chart** of your company, i.e. ***who does what***. Who takes care of the administration, of marketing, of sales, and so on. **Logistics** means which material goods you need, offices, equipment and machinery, sheds, and so on. Moreover, you have to describe your **company structure**, i.e. which legal formula you choose for your company, who forms it and how shares are distributed; for each associate you have to write down a biography that enhances the distinctive skills, saying what will each associate take care of, provided that there are other associates besides you. Indeed, we have already spoken about the negative aspects of having associates in your business.

The part that describes in detail the establishing of the company is a part that mostly interests **possible financiers** who want to assess the reliability of the company before investing in it. Financiers such as banks or private people will evaluate in detail not only the business idea, but also personally the associates of the company on which, of course, depend the success of the company itself and the return of their interests.

Probably the hardest part of all the business plan is the one related to the **financial forecasts**, in which you must also calculate the **Break Even Point**: the moment when you will get back all the investments you've made to start the company and you will start to go in the black. In this section you will have to forecast sales and sales volume, and this, for obvious reasons, it is really difficult.

This, roughly, is the structure of a business plan. It's clear that the more detailed the business plan, the better for you and for those who will evaluate it, such as banks or other potential financiers and business partners. Regardless of whether you need to apply for funding or seek capital partners, who will finance your business, I suggest you to write up a business plan. I speak frankly to you: this writing is not absolutely essential. Let's say that the business plan, however, may have **operative utility**, as it represents **a design element to which you can always refer**, although in time, due to the likely occurrence of not hypothesized events and factors, you will separate from it. So it's up to you whether to do it or not; I suggest you to do it, because ultimately you will stop to reflect on things that you had not thought, and so it will be useful anyway.

4.2. Where can you get the money?

Let's move on to a really classic and in some respects contradictory question. **Where do I get the money to start my business?** The theory teaches that you can find financiers (such as banks, relatives or friends), but that still means get into debts and then starting already in the red. You will always have someone who is breathing down your neck and your debts will weigh a ton.

Another alternative is looking for a partner or a capital partner, but in one way or another it will limit your own decision-making autonomy; you will have to share it with someone. I highly advise you against sharing your power with someone else. If you want to go out looking for associates or financiers, then prepare a good business plan, one that is *really* convincing. But now I tell you what I think. **Don't ask for money to anyone**, start from scratch making little steps, but betting everything on your own strength and on your resources. Don't make the mistake of getting into debts, but mostly **don't make the mistake of starting in grand style and biting off more than you can chew** if you have no experience. If you do, it is almost certain that you'll burn and fail. As the child begins to crawl, then walks, then runs, then rides a bike, then takes the license, you avoid rushing into things and do everything step by step. If you or your family don't have capitals, *money*, then try to **get them with your job.** Start saving and putting money aside to realize your dream. **Starting a business from scratch doesn't take a lot of money, especially if you operate on**

line. On the other hand, if your business requires substantial investments, then you should put away your dream for a while and start with an alternative business, which has the sole purpose of raising funds. Look around: there are so many ways to make money, of course I'm speak of legal ways. Start with an activity which, although it's not the one of your dreams, let you putting aside some money, so that it can fund the business of your dreams. Do some research and you'll see that there are safe ways to make money. When you have all the money you need, and especially if this money will be *yours*, hard-earned, you'll be much more motivated and much more conscientious and prudent in investing, and therefore unlikely you'll make a mistake. You'll also have done a little business experience, like it was a workout and a pre-season preparation. If, instead, you will start with someone else's money, you will begin very quickly doing things in grand style, running the risk of burning, making fatal mistakes due to inexperience. I suggest you to **think *always* big, but to take one step at a time, as all the greatest men did.** The success is not achieved by magic, but with so much effort and hard work. Remember the example of the plant that starts from a seed, becomes sprout, then shrub, then little plant, then sapling and finally fruit tree. Do not pretend that your seed generates directly a tree.

4.3. Startup: corporate form and first investments

Fundamental starting point is **what kind of company formula choose**. I suggest you to start with the cheapest and easiest one at fiscal level and then work up to the most important and challenging. Before you even set up the company, you can also test the market to assess the quality of your business.

For many types of business you can start even alone, without collaborators.

At first bend over backwards, work hard and try to do everything by yourself, so as not to have too many expenses. By the way, I confide you a big secret: **your first employee is the Internet.** Internet offers unlimited resources, you only need to take and exploit them. Internet connects you with an unlimited reservoir of people, resources and products, *free of charge*. Use it. Internet allows you even to **advertise at no cost,** thanks to advertisement websites. If you are looking for collaborators, uploading a simple free advert, the Internet will offer thousands of resumes. The Internet works for you, use it.

Starting by yourself, you will realize if your idea works and if your business produces. If you have worked well before, I'm sure it will. **At the beginning always invest all that you earn to make your business grow**. Don't be greedy and don't have the rush of wanting to immediately reap the benefits to put them aside and make money. Everything you gains should be invested for the growth of your business, but always making wise investments, without mistakes. Toiling for all the money from the beginning and having invested your direct resources will help you being very careful in investing, minimizing the possibility of error. As for your **private expenditures**, save as much as possible: eat bread and onion, don't go on holiday but, at first, dedicate all your resources to the development of your business, or it will always remain small and will never evolve. **Do you want to be rich?** Then you have to produce a successful business, but to do so your business needs to grow properly, and then you have to invest in it. I repeat, do not rush in reaping the benefits. At the beginning cut every superfluous expense, if you can; avoid, for example, to rent a luxurious office, rather work from home.

4.4. The magic word: *marketing*

Invest in marketing, to give visibility to your business. The more visibility, the more customers, the more sales volume, the sooner you'll become rich. I just quoted a magic word: *marketing*. Marketing is the art of selling, that is the power of making people buy your product or service. Learn to love this word and think constantly of it as the source of your earnings. Marketing must be your partner.

Today, there are basically **two types of marketing**: traditional marketing and Web marketing, which is the digital marketing.

Let's start from the **traditional marketing**; this means the promotion based on the means that were used exclusively before the birth of the Internet: radio, television, billposting, and so on. These are very expensive means and also have a major disadvantage: **they don't allow you to scientifically measure the ROI** (Return on Investment), i.e. their profitability, literally the economic return of the investment. ROI is the ratio of how much you have invested and how much you earn. If you invest in a television advertising campaign you'll spend a lot of money, you'll definitely have a lot of visibility and a good profit, but the problem is that you cannot scientifically measure this ratio. With the web marketing, instead, you can monitor ROI at any instant and **know how your advertising campaign is going. Web marketing**, being a form of digital promotion, offers you constantly statistics that you can analyze, correcting your promotional initiatives in real time. For an entrepreneur who starts from scratch this is the best form of marketing. I strongly recommend you get a culture on web marketing. Keep reading!

4.4.1. Different kind of web marketing: from pay-per-click to couponing

I describe some of the most common forms of web marketing. A classic form is the **pay-per-click** advertising through Google AdWords. Basically, you subscribe to digital marketing platform Google AdWords, creating one or more web marketing pay-per-click campaigns, that is, you pay only for clicks that your ads receive and which are a direct visit to your website by a potential customer. Using this service, Google will publish your ad on the front page, as if it were a search result on Google search engine. This guarantees you, with very low costs, immediate visibility on Google. You will choose a set of keywords, related to your business. For example, if your business is a **Sushi takeaway restaurant in Manhattan**, you'll write words like "sushi takeaway Manhattan", "Japanese food takeaway Manhattan", "takeaway Manhattan", and so on. All potential clients who will write these keywords on Google will find your ad on the front page and probably they will click on it, visiting your website, where they will probably make an order. So you will start earning right away. All this at a **modest sum**, since you'll pay only for the click you actually received, and consider that the cost of a click can range from a few cents to a few dollars, depending on the competition. Think about how much you will save compared to a promotional campaign via radio, television or billboards. If you don't believe me, try asking for quotes and then evaluate them. Not to mention that **today people search for almost**

everything on the Internet, since they have not only computers but also smartphones and tablets, and then people make research on the Internet not only from home, but wherever they are and at any time, 24/7. Think of how many clicks you can get with just $ 1,000 investment on Google AdWords.

Another winning form of web marketing is the **affiliation marketing**, which also allows you to use the formula "pay for performance". In this case, you don't even pay the clicks but you pay only if the sale took place. The platforms of affiliate marketing are based on this mechanism: you post your advertisement and a number of partners of the platform, which are affiliated to it, publish on their sites your ad. If a user, through an affiliate site, clicks on your ad and makes a sale, affiliates earn a percentage on the sale. So you have no fixed costs, but you pay only if you sell and then gain. Some very famous platforms of affiliation marketing are, for example, Zanox or Tradedoubler. You pay to the platform an activation cost for the service, and then you load a budget that, as you sell, will run out. These are two examples of web marketing that allow you to continuously monitor your ROI, i.e. the productivity of your advertising investment, through clicks and sales. If you're a new modern entrepreneur, you can't do without these opportunities.

Another form of web marketing is the **social media marketing**. It consists of investing in advertising campaigns on social media like Facebook, Twitter and LinkedIn, for example. In this case, you can decide whether to activate the **advertising campaigns for a fee**, through which you will only pay for each click your site will receive, or you can use social media making your advertising directly through activities on these sites, or viral videos. Speaking of which, another form of web marketing is the **viral marketing**. It consists in publishing on the Internet some videos or other "viral" contents, which have some peculiarities that lead them to a broad and spontaneous spread, potentially also on a global scale, through the sharing of content on the web, all for free. Think of those stupid video circulating on YouTube, which made people famous because they're funny, and have received millions of clicks. Forgive me if I speak of these arguments in a summary way, but each of them would deserve an entire book apart. Here I present you a catalog of the possibilities that will arise and that, as an entrepreneur, you are required to know.

Another secret of web marketing is **SEO**, or **"Search Engine Optimization".** This web marketing technique consists in making your website be positioned on first page on search engines. It takes place in two phases. The first step is to make your site *Google friendly*, i.e. optimize it for Google. The second step is to apply a *link building* strategy, which means that on many sites you publish a series of links and resources that generate traffic to your site. I don't go into technicalities because, also in this case, I should speak for dozens and dozens of pages. However, the purpose of SEO is to place your website on the front page in response to researches that concern a set of keywords, and I'm not talking about results sponsored by Google, in the formula of the pay-per-click with fee we've seen above, but about "organic" search results, which means "normal" and therefore free of charge; it is, in effect, free advertising. You can read up and do this work by yourself, becoming a good SEO, or paying a professional who will work for you by placing your site on Google for the commercial keywords you're interested in. In this way, you'll get visitors to your site *for free*, and you'll have a **free permanent advertising.**

Another very powerful web marketing form is **couponing**. You can partner with sites like Groupon or Groupalia, publishing coupon campaigns that will sell your product or your service; you'll directly acquire many customers, thanks to the visibility that these very famous sites will offer you, clearly in exchange for a portion of your earnings. Basically, they will do the marketing for you and procure many customers. Do not underestimate the power of partnerships, such as **licensing.** With this contractual formula you enter into a partnership, with which you acquire or give the right to commercial exploitation of a brand in exchange for royalties, which may be fixed or variable. Let's make an example. Instead of investing on building your own brand from scratch, which requires the investment of lots of time, effort and money, **you can buy someone else's brand**, and exploit it commercially. For example, if you want to sell covers for iPhone, you can buy, through a licensing agreement, the right to use some famous brands such as Disney or Marvel heroes, giving the licensee a percentage of sales or a flat fee for every sale. In this way, you can already benefit a strong brand, which doesn't need to be promoted because it's already famous, thus saving a lot of money in marketing. We can say that this can be a shortcut to do business, as Phil Knight did with Onitsuka Tiger, becoming the exclusive distributor in the United States, before founding the Nike brand.

4.4.2. Unconventional marketing

A form of not digital marketing, but still with a strong impact and equipped with the advantage of being low budget, is the **guerrilla marketing**. This form of marketing is so called because it is a bit borderline, in the sense that it is almost at the limit between the legal and not legal, so be careful. A case of guerrilla marketing that made history in Italy is related to the brand "**A-Style**". The A-Style logo depicts a stylized sexual intercourse. Since 1989, stickers depicting the logo were produced; they were applied around the Italian cities of Milan and Rome, and later also in Miami, Moscow and London. The brand was so strong that generated a great curiosity and a strong word of mouth, because it was really weird as it didn't led back to any company. **Only 10 years after its spread,** Marco Bruns founded the clothing company of the same name; it assured him a turnover of 20 million euros and it was a sponsor of MotoGP in 2007. This is a typical example of guerrilla marketing, i.e. a company that was born from scratch, spending very little money on marketing and simply thanks to a brilliant idea, widespread through word of mouth.

Another similar case is that of the youth apparel company "**Guru**". In 1999, the Italian Matteo Cambi draws the brand Guru, represented by a **stylized daisy.** As a frequenter of nightclubs in Milan, this young entrepreneur convinced the famous soccer player Christian Vieri, then at the peak of his career as a soccer player, to wear a guru t-shirt under the shirt of his team and to show its logo after every goal . This ensured to Cambi an extraordinary advertising, and soon he began to sell hundreds of thousands of t-shirts, bringing in 2006 the turnover of his company to 100 million euros. Also this story teaches us that starting from scratch, with very little investment and thanks to **unconventional marketing,** you can get to have a turnover of millions in no time.

I hope I've given you some good ideas for marketing; the burden of read up and learn about any subject of your interest is yours.

4.5. Delegate to get bigger: sellers, employees and co-workers

Another aspect of your business I want to talk about, and that you have to look after a lot, are **sales**, then the **commercial function**. If marketing comes first, sales come as second. When you won't be able to personally manage this aspect, look for the good sellers. They have to be very smart and motivated people, so do a good job of recruiting, preferably by linking them to your company with a fixed fee plus a variable on sales that they will achieve. They can make direct sales or secure distribution partnerships with other specialized companies. **Marketing and sales** are, for me, the most important functions of the company, as they **directly produce turnover**; for the rest, take always very care of the quality of your products and services, and of the **expertise of your staff**: follow them consistently and do it in person. When you'll grow up, learn to delegate work to people you trust, while always remaining in control of everything. **Have confidence in everyone but don't have blind confidence in anyone.** You must always keep in first person the control of your business. As you go forward, deal always of *business development*, delegating the practicality to your trusted employees. Although you start alone, slowly, automatically, you will be surrounded by a number of collaborators; so creates a hierarchy and an organization chart based on the concept of meritocracy and individual leadership, by always focusing on the concept of *team*, as everyone is always on the same boat and is sailing in the same direction.

I want to give you some advice about your **leadership.** Try to be a *captain* rather than a boss. The latter bases its power only on authority given by its position, while **the captain is always at the forefront, and bases its power on the respect that his employees have towards him.** While the boss is generally hated and criticized, the captain is a person worthy of respect, a true reference and model, an example to all on how to be at the forefront.

Always check maniacally every aspect of your business and never neglect any detail. Avoid any flaws to the edge that can take on board water, and remove as soon as possible the bad apples without hesitation. If you need to invest in consulting do it and **pick valuable consultants regardless of saving**: this is a safe investment that will bring you to grow. Remember that at the beginning, it's good doing it all alone, but then you have to learn to delegate in order to grow. If you want to do everything by yourself, you will always be small. Remember the example of the plant that from being seed then branches out: **you will be the trunk, but then there are the branches** that will bear fruit; **cut the branches that do not bear fruit**, and do it without hesitations. One thing is business and one other thing is friendship, love and family, so loved ones. **In business there are no loved ones but only money.** Learn to be cynical and unsentimental.

Finally, do not underestimate the power of market niches. If you're uncertain whether to bet on a mass market with high competition or on a **niche with great potential**, bet on the niche, where there is less competition but a lot of potential; you'll definitely have more and faster success.

That's all for now. I wish you to monetize the most my advice. In the last chapter we'll steal the secrets of great entrepreneurs who, starting from scratch, have become millionaires.

Good job my friend.

Secrets revealed in this chapter

- Starting a business from scratch doesn't take a lot of money, especially if you operate on line.
- Don't ask for money to anyone, but earn them with your job, or with an alternative activity.
- At the beginning always invest all that you earn to make your business grow.
- Cut all unnecessary expenses.
- The Internet works for you, use it.
- The more visibility, the more customers, the more sales volume, the sooner you'll become rich.
- Today people look for almost everything on the Internet: web marketing has to be your bread and butter.
- Work on SEO to get a free permanent advertising.
- Marketing and sales are the most important functions in a company, as they directly produce turnover.
- Have confidence in everyone but don't have blind confidence in anyone.
- Be a *captain* rather than a boss: the captain is always at the forefront, and bases its power on the respect that his employees have towards him.
- Delegate in order to grow up.

5. LET'S LEARN THE SECRETS FROM NEW MILLIONAIRE ENTREPRENEURS THAT HAD STARTED FROM SCRATCH

In this chapter, I'll tell you stories of incredible success of the great entrepreneurs of our time, soon became millionaires starting from scratch. Something to think about is the fact that most of them are young and **have made their fortune with on line business.**

5.1. Andrew Mason - Groupon

First story I tell you is the one of Andrew Mason, founder of Groupon.

Groupon is the world leader in couponing, a system of on line offers, that signed partnerships with companies that offer deep discounts on their products and services in exchange for a commission of 50%, held back from Groupon. Groupon has had a worldwide hit, as it offers excellent business offering products and services discounted up to 90%, something never seen before. The company that publishes an offer on Groupon is sure to find many customers and a great on line visibility.

Mason, born in 1980, at the age of 15 had founded his first business, a service of home delivery at a local level, the "Bagel Express." In 2008 he founded Groupon taking it, after only two years, **from zero to $ 800 million in turnover**. An incredible boom, a real business case, with a rapid worldwide spread. In 2010, **Google offers $ 6 billion to buy Groupon but this offer is rejected:** Mason doesn't want to sell. In 2011 Groupon is quoted on the Stock Exchange. In the meanwhile all over the world are born many couponing companies, clones and followers of Groupon, including the Spanish **Groupalia**. These inevitably steal significant market share from Groupon. Thus, in 2013, Mason was fired as CEO of Groupon, as analysts' sales expectations were no confirmed. A sad fate, which recalls the story of Steve Jobs when he was fired from Apple, before of coming back in a big way, starting a new era for the company of Cupertino.

Let's analyze this case in detail. **What are the credits and what are the mistakes of Mason?** Among the credits, the one of being a great visionary and innovator who knew how to ride the trend in the expansion of e-commerce. In addition, he has launched this business, based on an **aggressive discount system**, exactly when the world was facing an economic crisis, and so this kind of service has immediately achieved an incredible success and sparked a viral word of mouth that has brought it in a few years to be worthed $ 6 billion. So, in addition of being a visionary, Mason is also the figure of entrepreneur with a great eye and great timing, as well as being definitely a very good organizer and manager.

What did he get wrong, therefore, to be fired by the company he founded after just five years? He basically get two things wrong. He had to realize that **the success of his company was the son of a particular historical moment** that could not last forever; in addition, if at the beginning he had the monopoly of the market he invented, after a short time he began to suffer from fierce competition from numerous competitors who cloned his business, nibbling more and more market shares. So Mason had to realize that **his parabola could not grow forever**, but that **sooner or later it would begin to decline**. It's like a roulette player at the casino who can't get up from the table while he's winning, but he keeps playing until he loses everything. Are we quite sure that he would not have agreed to accept $ 6 billion from Google? Starting from scratch and selling your own business for 6 billion after only two years is not that bad after all.

Besides, he made a rather controversial choice, that is quoting his company on the Stock Exchange. By doing that **you lose the absolute power over your company.** Many successful entrepreneurs choose not to *ever* go public on the stock market, as Kamprad did for Ikea, which despite everything is still a family business. When you bring your company in the Stock market, you become a leader like everyone else, and shareholders in the event of failure, can fire you, as happened to Jobs and Mason. Being kicked out of your own home, honestly, it's a very sad thing. Consider that it is normal for a company to have ups and downs, but if you are the owner then you can easily ride over a moment of storm; if, instead, you give the power to **shareholders, they will kick you out at the first opportunity, because you are a too big and powerful character.** Think about this case, regardless of the company proportions.

5.2. Brian Chesky - Airbnb

The story of Brian Chesky is very special and it really makes you think for several reasons. Chesky was born in 1981 and had the idea of founding Airbnb in 2008, by chance. At the time, Chesky was living in San Francisco, where he shared an apartment with other people. **During the period when the famous design exhibition in San Francisco was held, all the hotels were sold out,** so he decided to temporarily rent his home getting a nice gain.So, just by chance, it was born the idea of **an on line service that would put directly in contact individuals who want to sublet their homes and individuals who need a temporary accommodation.** You can sublet a room, a sofa or even an inflatable air mattress on the floor, hence the term *air bed and breakfast.* Thanks to this as banal as brilliant, simple idea, this guy has invented a multi-million dollar global business. This new service not only did the fortunes of its founder in economic terms, but also revolutionized a static industry such as hotels, offering a new opportunity for temporary accommodation to millions of tourists, at low cost and, possibly, at direct contact with people from different cultures.

After one year, Chesky had 15 employees who worked in his apartment; **he even sacrificed his own bedroom** and had to go to sleep at other site members' houses. Today Airbnb has made the history of the hospitality and tourism industry; it's constantly developing and increasing its sales and it generated many clones. For us, however, is proof that

you can invent a millionaire business even from a relatively trivial idea, you just need to want it.

I give you a millionaire idea. Think of a sort of Airbnb for cars. It wold revolutionize the private transport system.

5.3. Drew Houston - Dropbox

Houston is a boy born in 1983 that in 2007, at the age of 24, founded the revolutionary on line service Dropbox. This on line service gives its users, *for free*, space *in cloud* to store their data using dedicated servers. Basically, the user signs up to Dropbox and he has the right of some gigs of free space, which allows him to store his files, creating normal files. In turn, he can invite other users and thanks to their registrations he will gain additional on line space. The story goes that Houston has invented Dropbox because, **as a student, he was tired of forgetting always his flash drive,** so he decided to create an on line space on which to store his data, as he may have access to them from any terminal with a simple login .Since the idea was very useful and functional for him, Houston thought then to extend it to the world and also he entered the club of millionaires entrepreneurs started from scratch, and, I add, *very young*. This story teaches us that, often, **million dollar ideas can arrive simply working *on your own needs***, which are at 99% the same as everyone else. Thus, the millionaire entrepreneur challenge lies also in the fact of being able to understand and interpret the new needs of the people, turning them into millionaire business.

5.4. Jack Dorsey - Twitter

Jack Dorsey is the American entrepreneur who founded Twitter in 2006, at the age of 30. As entrepreneur he made his debut at the age of 15, creating a company to manage transport services locally. He also belongs to the group of entrepreneurs that, having started a big business, no longer have finished their studies.

The idea of Twitter stems from the desire to **share his own status *instantly* with his friends**. Please note, Twitter was born two years after Facebook. This means that Jack Dorsey didn't think about competition problems, such as an inferiority complex or simply about having started his business after Facebook. So Twitter, in a very short time, became leader of *micro blogging* and a powerful on line media. Consider **Twitter, from a technological point of view, is much simpler than Facebook as it offers only a very small part of the features that Facebook offers.** Yet **people like it because of this**, generating millions of "Twitter evangelists" who prefer it to Facebook, insulting even the rival and its users. Twitter comes to the fore thanks to the 2008 presidential election in the United States, as it is used by both Obama and McCain to update their supporters. Then, in this case, it becomes not just a tool of mass communication but also of political marketing. The phenomenon occurs again on an even higher scale in 2009, in Iran, causing even the civil revolution. In this case, indeed, it is not used by politicians, but by common people who, **thanks to Twitter, spread the word of the revolt in the**

world. Same thing will happen in the following years in other parts of the world.

Twitter makes us think, because it teaches us that, starting from a simple idea, you can become a millionaire and you can make even the history of the world. Twitter, like Facebook, **isn't a profit-making business, but with the introduction of advertising, is a millionaire business** that in 2011 was estimated 4 billion dollars.

5.5. Jeff Bezos - Amazon

Bezos was born in 1964 and in 1994, at the age of 30, **he founded in his garage Amazon**, sensing the trend of e-commerce and seizing opportunity by the rapid growth of the Internet. To build Amazon from scratch, he leaves his well-paid job and all his economic certainties, blindly believing in the business that would bring him to eternal glory, and to be one of the richest men in the world. Today, Amazon is the e-commerce leader, having almost reached a position of monopoly. He began by selling books, but now he sells almost everything. However, the trend of **e-commerce** is still at the beginning and is constantly developing, so **it is still a great time to invest in innovative businesses in this sector.** It's okay to innovate, but it's also okay to simply **create a niche**, as **Zalando** has done, becoming the European leader in the sale of shoes and accessories. Bezos, as Jobs, is described as a manic for the care with which he follows all the details of his companies, and he is famous for some motto, such as: "the most dangerous thing is not evolving" and "there are two kinds of companies, those that work to try to raise their prices and those that work to try to lower them. We are the second kind". This second motto is very similar to the philosophy of Ikea.

Today, Bezos aims to invest in the field of intergalactic travels, that is in space tourism, as his illustrious colleague Branson who founded the Virgin Galactic. From this point of view, these two immense entrepreneurs prove themselves as great visionaries, simply anticipating what the future will be.

5.6. Reid Hoffman - LinkedIn

Hoffman, was born in America in 1967 and is one of the most important entrepreneurs in the history of the Internet. He is famous as the co-founder of LinkedIn, that was founded in 2003, a year before Facebook and three years before Twitter. Consider that, when it was created, this professional networking service **was so far ahead that it was hard to understand.** Today, it's an essential tool for all workers of the world, and has a value that goes far beyond 10 billion dollars. Hoffman is considered one of the greatest visionary entrepreneurs of the Internet and he has had a key role in the merger of PayPal and eBay. He is also one of the greatest *angel investor* over the last 10 years, having invested in over 80 web startups companies, including Facebook, Digg and Zynga. Having created LinkedIn before Facebook and Twitter, we can define Hoffman a great innovator and visionary. Today is one of the most powerful men in the world.

5.7. Pierre Omidyar - eBay

Born in 1967 in Paris, later naturalized American, Omidyar is the founder of eBay, the famous on line auction site as well as the most important e-commerce site in the world. He began working on the eBay project in 1995 at the age of 28. The service begins immediately to be highly fruitful; so, in 1997, it was given the final name of eBay. The slogan of this site is "**whatever you're looking for is on eBay**" and it is really so. EBay has revolutionized the world of business, both locally and globally and has had a very rapid diffusion on a global scale. Its founder has certainly been **an entrepreneur very attentive to trends**, visionary because he strongly believed in his project, creating one of the most visited websites in the world. He is now one of the richest men in the world and is also a great philanthropist.

5.8. Matt Mullenweg - Wordpress

Born in 1984, Mullenweg is the founder of WordPress, the software platform for *personal publishing and content management system* (CMS) the most widespread in the world.**WordPress bases its success on ease of use, allowing anyone to build a website on his own, in few minutes, for free.** WordPress was born in 2003, when its founder was only 19. Mullenweg was definitely an entrepreneur prodigy, but also a visionary and a philanthropist, as he has innovated the way people communicate on the Internet, allowing anyone to create their own website easily and for free and that was very hard before WordPress. So, let's think of the impact that WordPress has had on the economy. These stories teach us that you can be a great millionaires entrepreneur and a philanthropist at the same time, creating services that could help people.

5.9. David Karp - Tumblr

Karp, born in 1986, is the young founder of Tumbrl. This on line platform was created **in 2007, when its founder was just 21 years old.** It's a social networking and microblogging platform, which in 2013 was sold to Yahoo for 1.1 billion dollars. In this same year, Tumblr is home of 108 million blogs.

This story makes us think for two reasons: first, **it's never too soon to become entrepreneurs.** Second, if we want to focus on **an area where there are already the big names**, as Karp did in social networking and microblogging, don't think of any problem or hesitation: *let's act.* Do you believe that the nineteen-year-old Karp has been frightened by the idea of dealing with Facebook, Twitter, WordPress? Absolutely not, and after a few years he became a billion dollars entrepreneur.

Moral: it is never too soon, just do it.

5.10. Blake Ross - Mozilla

Ross, born in 1985, is one of the founders of Mozilla Firefox. He was a child prodigy when **at the age of 10 made his first website.** When he was 14, he worked as an intern at Netscape, the first major browser with a global reach. In 2003, at the age of 18, he is a co-founder of **Mozilla Firefox, the open source browser that very quickly spread around the world**, stealing significant market share in the monopoly of Microsoft Internet Explorer. The challenge between Mozilla and Internet Explorer is a bit like the classic David against Goliath: **it seems almost impossible for a small man to fight a giant with disproportionate force.** But Firefox has been the demonstration that no market challenge is impossible. Even competing with weapons much lower, in fact, Firefox has even managed to become the first-ever web browser in some countries such as Germany. Speaking of *nothing is impossible.*

5.11. Shawn Fanning - Napster

Let's conclude our overview of young, big millionaires entrepreneurs who started from scratch with on line business, telling the story of Fanning, founder of the legendary Napster. This guy that was born in 1980, founded, in 1999, **Napster, which was one of the first p*eer-to-peer* platforms in the world.** This project collected in a very short time so much of popularity that it was dedicated to Fanning even a cover of the magazine "Time". Unfortunately, for legal reasons derived from copyright law, Napster was shut down in 2001. After this experience, which has made the history of the Internet contributing to its spread in the world, Fanning has continued to work in the world of the Web as an entrepreneur and *angel investor*. This story teaches us that we can become myths of entrepreneurship even with borderline projects, i.e. on the borders of illegal, as the young "pirate" Fanning did.

Arriving to the conclusions of this chapter, we can say that it's never too soon to start your own successful project, but you have to believe blindly in it against all odds, always fighting and acting without hesitation and fear; you have to go straight to the realization of your dreams, beyond the generic appearance of your ideas. **Even seemingly trivial idea, in fact, can make us millionaires entrepreneurs from scratch**, as history teaches us.

Secrets revealed in this chapter

- Your business curve can't grow forever; sooner or later it may start a decline.
- Don't lose the absolute power over your company.
- You can invent a millionaire business even from a relatively trivial idea.
- Million dollar ideas can arrive simply working on *your own* needs, which are at 99% the same as everyone else.
- A successful business can paradoxically offer less functionality than a similar one that already exists, just simplifying it.
- Even not profit-making business may, with the introduction of advertising, become millionaire business.
- It's okay to innovate, but it's also okay to create a niche.
- *People don't want to have difficulty*: many successful business are based on ease of use, a simplicity that have to be available to everyone.
- It's never too soon to become entrepreneurs.
- Do not be afraid of facing the giants in your industry: *they will be afraid* of you!

6. CONCLUSIONS I GIVE YOU SOME MILLIONAIRE IDEAS

Let's start with a premise: **everyone can be millionaire**, if he wants to and he wishes it firmly. The first secret that you have learned by now reading the previous chapters of this book, is that to become a millionaire you only need to want it and believe it with all of yourself. An assumption is surely think positively, think big and be able to master your fears and weaknesses. The secret of positive thinking is, to quote the Italian self made millionaire entrepreneur, Silvio Berlusconi, "**to have the sun in your pocket**," a tremensdous willpower and to be able to withstand adversities when they arise, knowing how to overcome obstacles as a navigator during a storm. The captain of a ship that faces a long sea voyage already knows that, along his routes, he might meet with storms and very high waves; he must, however, bravely face them and overcome them, because after the storm there is always clear sky. All difficulties we may encounter are part of the game, but the good navigator, like the great entrepreneur, knows hot to resist the difficulties and overcome them.

Having the sun in your pocket means **being equipped with an innate and certain optimism that must be contagious for ourselves and for others**, that is for the people we involve in our projects and will work with us to achieve our dreams, to achieve our major goals. Optimism is something that shines through our ideas, our projects and that will be contagious to those around us, whether they are employees, financiers, customers or potential customers.

In this chapter I will give you some **ideas to make a great millionaire business**. Always remember that no matter what you do, as with every startup, you have to realize it starting from scratch; don't let the need of starting small scares you, because so all the greatest ones did, like Steve Jobs who has built Apple starting from the home of his partner Wozniak or like Page who started Google from a garage.

We have already said that the great entrepreneur has nose and can read the reality, understanding what are the opportunities for the future. You must know then take trends and imagine the more distant future.

In the previous chapter we have also seen that **all of the latest big millionaires started from scratch did it with the Internet-based projects.** So there is no doubt that today you should focus on the web to build possible financial empires. After all, the web is still at its beginnings, despite what people may think. Recently people talked about a ***2.0 Internet era***: this same definition is the confirmation that we are, after all, still at the beginnings.

6.1. Hunger for communication

One of the growing trends is that of **interpersonal and global communication.** The Internet, thanks to some social network platforms, has been in touch in real time with people all over the world and this was a great cultural revolution, a kind of **Copernican revolution of communication.** The Internet has broken down the concept of passive communication of yore, based on the *passive* use of means of mass communication. The Internet has spread instead a **"rhizomatic" communication**, which means devoid of a true center of the spread of the communication and of its imposed passive use, but in which each subject is in turn mean of the global spread of communication. Let's pause a moment to think about what is the current state of communication based on nowadays social networks. With Facebook or Twitter every person can, by his own personal space, communicate with the whole world. But **how will be the Facebook and Twitter of the future?** You have to consider that they are now so big and strong and with a structural identity so marked, that they will actually remain similar to themselves, not being able to easily evolve; so that, with the gradual creation of new models of communication due to the evolution of technology, the same Facebook and Twitter need to be updated quickly or they'll risk being overtaken by new communication models and new platforms.

For example, with the spread of broadband and more and more powerful technological tools, we will be able to communicate in an ever more complex way, perhaps using **publishable video in streaming in real time**, as if it were a live recording, like a webcam.

While today we communicate on Twitter and Facebook by writing, in the near future we will **directly leave voice messages** or even recorded or live video messages. Everyone will have access to his own space and communicate through video or through voice, as if he was a radio speaker. These are ideas that you can understand and develop on your own. Think about when, in the 70s, private radio stations and local radios, started from the homes of amateur spread. Those ones, with rudimentary equipment, could broadcast their radio communications with a clearly limited range and on a local scale. This was one of the first cultural revolution because, **in a time far away from the web**, everyone could, with little means, communicate to an audience of strangers, using radio technology. In some cases, thanks to the entrepreneurial spirit of some of them, these radios have evolved into national networks, able to make an turnover of millions of dollars in advertising and give jobs to thousands of employees. Today, with the Internet, it can happen the same thing but using a digital medium. Let's think of Facebook and Twitter of the future and of the more and more powerful digital technology opportunities and **design your own social network project**; you only have to do it. Do not set limits or restrictions: think big and take the opportunity to reach global audiences; do not think anymore on local scale, because this is an anachronism, but **think directly of the whole world**. Think that the **drug of the**

future is communication and thanks to the new tools the new generations are addicted to communication; they are *hypercommunicative.* With this I'm saying that they have hunger for communication and they look forward to discover new resources and new platforms, more and more advanced, to communicate.

Facebook and Twitter also have **revolutionized the concept of personal privacy**, stimulating that **desire that everyone has of sharing with the world every detail of his life**, all his experiences. People want anything but to do so in a more and more powerful, fast and effective way. Think about how to do it and give the, this great opportunity before others do.

So, the first key concept is to develop and do business on the hunger for communication people have and on this point, despite appearances, we still are at the beginning.

Force yourself to consistently do this meditation exercise, to become visionaries: you have to imagine how the world will look like in 100 years and **design innovative services *today*.** Don't focus on what already exists, do not just think about how to improve it but look over it. If you focus only on a slow and gradual improvement of the existing, you will end up being just followers, that is entrepreneurs who focus their energies in doing something that, just as is done, will have already been passed elsewhere by someone else. Therefore you have to look so far ahead: *this* means being visionary; never set limits to the imagination. Nothing is impossible. Get always inspiration from the greats, such as

Leonardo da Vinci and Steve Jobs, great innovators and visionaries of their time.

In summary, again citing Jobs, "**think different**", detach from the obvious and from how others think; they think of the present, you think of the future, look beyond. To win you have to be a radical innovator.

6.2. Hunger for knowledge

In addition to the hunger for communication, people have also **hunger for knowledge.**

Before knowledge was something for a few, something that cost much. School costs, professors cost, books cost. **The Internet has revolutionized the knowledge**, making it available to everyone and pooling all the information on the network. But even here we are only at the beginning. Think of how much **Wikipedia** has given to the world, as free and produced-by-people encyclopedia. It feeds on knowledge not imposed from above, but spread from the base, i.e. by network users on a voluntary basis, free of charge. The same assumption pools those families of knowledge and spontaneous information that are the several **thematic forums disseminated in the network.** Or the popular information system of **Yahoo Answers**. But think about the *limits* of this information. Do you realize how much time you lose in the search for information in various forums and sites, very often running into useless answers and false information? Well, think about the way these platforms evolve and how the knowledge in the future will spread. Can you **imagine a site for answers**, for example? That is, a search engine that, unlike Google which offers various results through an index of sites, may instead already **summarize the contents within a single site**, taking the various information from the network? Like a robot that collects information for you, without you having to read the various sites, but making you a summary of the information that you need. Do you think this is impossible? Do you think this will not happen in the future? I think that you're *wrong.* Prejudices and self-limitations are the first enemies for visionary entrepreneur. After all, **the old YouTube** is just a trivial video picker. **Nothing is revolutionary until it is created.** With the Internet you don't have to invent astrophysical formulas, but create digital systems and services. Stop and make right now a brainstorming thinking about the future Internet. Write on a piece of paper all the ideas that come to your mind, from the most banal to the most insane... surely something good will come out. Be careful, I don't mean that you have to invent something incredible; that is the visionary job, you can simply create a winning service that works on a global scale, *radically* improving something that already exists. For example, think about the e-commerce trend ... and follow me to the last paragraph of the book.

6.3. Crazy about e-commerce

Think of that madman who, as first, had the **idea of selling shoes on the Internet.** It seems crazy to sell something on the Internet that traditionally you have to try it for yourself in a shop, checking if it fits perfectly on your foot. This is the story of Robert Gentz and David Schneider, founders of the German **Zalando**, an European leader in e-commerce of shoes and accessories, founded in 2008.**How many insults these two have received**, when initially spoke of their idea with friends and family? The solution is simply to ***take the side of the consumer:*** if the shoe you get home doesn't fit, you send it to the sender without losing your money. So, from a senseless idea it was born a millionaire business. Think about it.

If all business will move sooner or later on the Internet, and this is the future, how many areas still don't have a corresponding digital display, a system of distribution and sale on the net? What are the unspoken potentialities of e-commerce? It seems so absurd that, **one day not too far away, people will buy exclusively on the Internet?** I bet this is the future.

As you can see, the space of action is basically unlimited.

I simply wish you good job.

Secrets revealed in this chapter

- Always brings the sun with you, in your pockets.
- The millionaire entrepreneur must have an innate and convinced optimism, that must be contagious for ourselves and for others.
- Imagine how the world will look like in 100 years, and design innovative services *today.*
- The drug of the future is communication.
- People are hungry for knowledge, or rather the *possibility* of knowledge.
- Nothing is revolutionary until it is created.
- You must be on the consumer side.
- In today's reality is written the future.

Printed in Great Britain
by Amazon